Fish On!
(Secrets of the Snook Whisperer)

Sloane Golden -
The Existential Angler

AuthorHouse™
1663 Liberty Drive, Suite 200
Bloomington, IN 47403
www.authorhouse.com
Phone: 1-800-839-8640

© 2008 Sloane Golden - The Existential Angler. All rights reserved.

No part of this book may be reproduced, stored in a retrieval system, or transmitted by any means without the written permission of the author.

First published by AuthorHouse 3/8/2008

ISBN: 978-1-4343-5360-3 (sc)
ISBN: 978-1-4343-6335-0 (hc)

Library of Congress Control Number: 2007909103

Printed in the United States of America
Bloomington, Indiana

This book is printed on acid-free paper.

-TO SKY & PHOEBE, FISHER-KIDS

Foreward:

Fishing, like any sport, is a testament to character. Win or lose, a fisherman must learn to overcome adversity and fish on to land the fish, achieve a goal, or a dream and take home the championship trophy. It takes more than luck and skill. It takes patience, determination and discipline—all virtues, which fishing teaches. As Coach of the world champion Tampa Bay Lightning, I can tell you it takes more than luck to win the championship. It takes the desire to understand every aspect of the game, the details large or small. As in ice-hockey, so it is in fishing. The basic rules apply. A champion fisherman must first learn the rules of the fishing game to succeed: when and where to use what bait and tackle, how to fish the water columns, how to target specific species, and last but certainly not least- how to tie a knot that will stand the test. Above all—you must first have a dream, then be prepared, focused, driven to excel. And I am still a student of the game!

To me, fishing is like an island of peace in the tempest of sport. In our championship season, we had to overcome many obstacles to win the biggest prize in hockey- The Stanley Cup. Fishing gives me time to relax and un-wind, amid the fast-paced stress and strife of coaching and career; time to stop and enjoy the simple things in life. Whether it's fishing or coaching, I play to win. From my kayak, or fresh-water fishing at our Wisconsin Lake, fishing is a way to hear my own heartbeat—to have fun and feel like a kid again. It motivates and inspires me to play on.

Sloane Golden, the Snook Whisperer, in his book, Fish On—shows the fisherman how to dream big and catch big fish. But the book is about more than fishing, however; it's about the test of character, something every winner must have. Part motivational, part inspirational, the book serves as a practical guide to the rules of the game, and understanding the game is the first step to mastering any sport, to become a true champion, to win and win big in any arena, on land, at sea or on the ice.

- Coach, John Tortorella,
Coach of the world champion Tampa Bay Lightning.

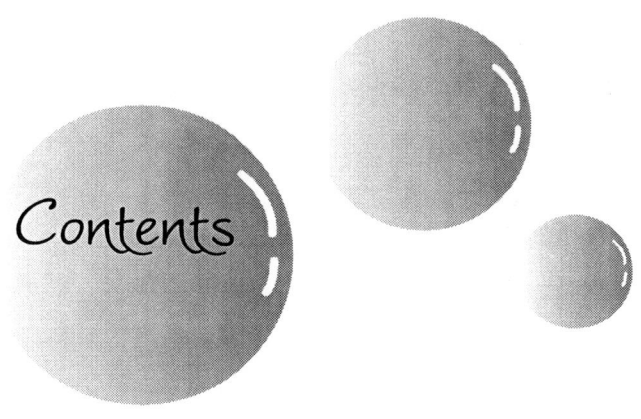

Contents

1 Storm Warning..9
2 Heart of a Champion: Lesson Of The Bonita..........17
3 Dreaming Of The Big One: Lesson Of The Snook......29
4 Take Your Kids Fishing On A Star...................37
5 On The Rocks: Lesson Of The Lowly Pinfish.........43
6 Eye Of The Storm...................................55
7 Flat-line: Lesson Of The Flats.....................59
8 Knee Deep In It: Lesson Of The Ladyfish............63
9 The Snook Whisperer................................71
10 Black Spot: Lesson Of The Redfish..................81
11 Dark Matter.......................................101
12 "Fear Itself": Lesson Of The Shark................109
13 "Sea School": Lesson Of The Hammerhead............117
14 The Turning Of The Tide: Lesson Of The Tides......123
15 Of Knots, The Ties That Bind......................129
16 Losing Heart: The Death of Dogs...................143
17 Lesson Of The Strike Zone.........................151

18	Land's End: Lesson Of The Cobia	161
19	Last Ticket To Paradise	171
20	Of Fisherman And Fools	175
21	A Fish Story: In Memory Of Elizabeth Reed	185
22	Swimming With The Sharks: In Hollywood	191
23	Today's The Day	199
24	If Love Were All	207
25	Silver Kings: Lesson Of The Tarpon	211
26	Bluewater: Lesson Of The Marlin	217
27	Calling The Spirit Down: I, Fisherman	223

Introduction: Fish + On!

With its winding, graceful scimitar of coastline, incised—like a laser cut—from the Gulf into an improbable peninsula of land, Florida lies like a giant reef in the epi-center of the sea- the fishing capital of the world.

Offshore, from Tarpon to Tiger Sharks, from Sailfish to Marlin, Barracuda, Wahoo, and Tuna, the Florida angler has his choice; inshore - the angler may land an Inshore Slam: Snook, Redfish and Trout, or down among the shimmering shallows of the Keys—a gray ghost known as the Bonefish, a species which many call the most elusive and challenging of all.

Curving west through iridescent blue-green waters, the archipelago of the Florida Keys offers world class sport-fishing. A drive down US Highway 1, the oldest highway in America, leads to Islamorada, Marathon, the Matecumbes and Key West. Presently, the Keys hold 146 fishing world records, more than any other single location on earth.

Want a shot at Blue Marlin, sailfish, Wahoo, kingfish, yellow or black-fin tuna? A world class fishery lies 75-125 miles offshore from the west central coast of Florida. The Loop abounds with pelagic fishing of every variety.

Into the immense open spaces of the Gulf Stream, an Angler may follow the path of the Loop Current, as he trolls for Blue and White Marlin, schools of Kingfish, and Cobia and Amberjack, among the reefs and shipwrecks, drifting on the trade winds, as flocks of migratory birds measure the beat of their wings in slow flight against a big blue sky.

Farther North, up Highway 1 lies the Everglades, lonely forgotten reaches of un-fished waters, where the sky and the water seem to merge into one, and a kayaker might easily disappear down Lost Man's River in search of exceptionally large, almost prehistoric Snook, during the Snook spawn, May through October.

Up the east coast lies the epicenter of world Tarpon fishing: Boca Grande Pass. In April and early May through mid-June, the Tarpon migration is legendary, as thousands of Silver Kings thrash their way through the pass. Once hooked, they leap from the water, flashing in the sun, giving them their distinctive nickname-the Silver King.

Last but not least, there is a little jetty, where on certain rare and magical occasions, when you call the Spirit down you may catch all of the above and more- in one day.

Through red tides and hurricanes, terrorist threats and political maelstroms, Florida has drunk from the fabled fountain of youth and has kept its spirit eternally young as only fishing can keep you young. For fishing is a thing of the Spirit; it grants you second sight-the ability to see beneath the surface into the deeper things of life, into a purpose in eternity.

Fish on, Florida!

1 Storm Warning

Alone at first light or at the close of day, fishing for speckled trout, salt-silvered by the dawn; stalking a pod of redfish along the edges of an oyster bar, as their tails ripple the water like the first raindrops beginning to fall; stalking a Linesider, amid the sultry summer Mangroves, as the lightning unfurls above your head, and your drag begins to sing; or further out, Blue Marlin, dappled lavender in the morning sun, tail-walking across the waves; the diabolical fury of a hooked shark beneath the Skyway, the reel ratcheting into a long mechanical wail, line running out, with a power that's impossible to check; or a Tarpon, from your Kayak—and a Hammerhead as big as a VW van moving in for the kill-- whatever a fisherman's passion— Florida has it all and more.

Just remember to watch out for the hurricanes.

For when the hard winds of change begin to blow through your life, they carry away a lot of the load you once thought of as important, permanent, stable– exposing, amid the wreckage, the essential things that truly matter. And questions, which you once thought easily answerable, suddenly become bottomless. Such were the difficult years between 2003 and 2005, when eight hurricanes ravaged the state of Florida, (including a brush with Katrina) when my life also experienced a continuous storm front, which threatened to wipe me from the face of the earth: I lost my job, got divorced, and my father came home to die, his body ravaged by cancer, lymphoma, to be exact.

Chemotherapy had crippled his immune system and left his spirit crushed - on the brink of a dark abyss. He was a permanent invalid, unable to move or fend for himself. He had come home a ruined, wasted man.

After falling out of bed and breaking his rib at what was euphemistically entitled a "retirement home," I was chosen to become his care-taker. I fed him, bathed him, and struggled to keep his spirits up.

To watch one's father expire before one's eyes shakes the foundations of everything you believe in. All your idols crumble into dust. In the end you face it alone. There's no other way. Yet there is comfort —even joy to be found amid the storm—in the simple things, such as fishing.

The two D's it seems, death and divorce, almost inevitably appear together. Add to the mix several hurricanes, in as many months, and you have a life torn apart. My life as I had known it came to an abrupt and sudden end in May 2003.

Only one thing saved me from despair.

Something long buried from a forgotten past—something the storms dredged up. Something I had once been very good at in childhood—lucky, charmed even, and which in the intervening years of marriage and career, had become less important until it seemed a part of an enchanted childhood, far, far away, and which when I reclaimed it, seemed almost like a miracle.

I became a born-again fisherman. Along the way I learned the many practical, down to earth lessons, which only fishing has to teach. I learned to comprehend and anticipate the monthly lunar cycles and its effect on the tides; I learned to read the water, not just the surface, but the water columns, like some people read the pages of a book.

I learned the lesson, which every species of fish has to teach, from bait to lures, from how, when and where to fish in the water column—and I learned to live again.

I learned the virtues of patience and discipline, and 100 miles out – blue water fishing in the Loop Current of the Gulf Stream, I learned humility, to let go of things beyond my control. This was, in many ways, the most life-changing lesson of all.

I also learned to tie a series of fisherman's knots: to fasten line to line, leader to line and hook to line to hold the biggest fish fast, which in turn offered me valuable instruction about life, especially the meaning of bonds and family ties. From this I learned the difference between a friend and an acquaintance.

You may meet a stranger and after twenty minutes, he becomes a life-long friend, or know an acquaintance for twenty years, and he remains just that--an acquaintance. The difference is the knot, the bond you make or fail to make. Do all tag ends meet and connect to form a lasting relationship, or does the knot slip and the relationship fade away? The difference is in the care of the knot you tie.

One of the most significant lessons was driven home one day under a bridge in Islamorada, Key West, when I went Tarpon fishing in a Kayak and was pulled out to sea. Alone on the water, surrounded by sharks – I learned to fish on in the face of fear and long odds, to maintain my equilibrium both in fishing and in life, and though I was to lose that fight to a giant hammerhead –I learned something indispensable: to lose, but not to be defeated by it.

Death leaves one vulnerable, in a constant, vague state of dread, which under the duress of imminent loss, leads to an overwhelming sense of loss. With that loss comes a loss of control over life itself, and with that, a loss of identity.

All of which is terribly difficult to live with; it's like a clock has wound down, the hands are broken, frozen in place, but time moves on without you. And you're helpless to do anything about it. There you stand, a broken clock with broken hands, and no one to fix it.

The diagnosis of my father's cancer left me unable to eat or sleep; worse, with an irregular heartbeat, which worried me. I too, felt death's unfinished business brushing by—close, too close. Like maybe his overnight bag was packed for two. As I lived each day, I endured a low-key sense of quiet desperation, which never left me, except when I was fishing.

One day I started painting my house. I painted one wall, before I realized the paint was the wrong color. On my way to the hardware store to exchange the paint, I had to pull over because the tears in my eyes were blinding me, and I could no longer see the road.

I swerved into a ditch, the can tipped over and paint gurgled all over the carpet of my 4 Runner. I could not enter the store in this state, so I limped home, sat down in the middle of my half-painted house and wept, the sobs echoing through the empty rooms. The worst—and the best were yet to come.

In an excellent anthology, "Hemingway On Fishing," a little tome of literary excerpts, in which the author's works on fishing are intertwined with his fiction, Hemmingway uses fishing as a metaphor to stave off death. I made the short story, "Now I Lay Me," my own. In it, a young protagonist, wounded at night in the war, listens to a silk-worm in his room, which he associates with a symbol of death, and re-lives his trout fishing days as a boy to allay his fears of dying in his sleep.

Amazing how much of Hemingway's artistic opus is coupled with his love of fishing in juxtaposition with the proximity of death. The theme runs throughout almost every work of his, major and minor, including my favorite, "The Old Man and The Sea."

I borrowed Hemmingway's technique, and whenever things got bad in the sleepless, soul-searching hours, between mid-night and the false gray dawn, I too used fishing as my refuge, re-living every moment of my past and present spent fishing.

I replayed every moment of the day in my mind; ritualistically I re-tied the knots, baited the hook, cast my line out, the rod being an extension of my soul, into the sea.

With each cast I sent out a prayer to something larger than myself, which hopefully cared what happened to me, something or someone who understood my fears, someone who would favor me with a reply – God provides the fish, and by extension, tugs on the other end of my line, letting me know someone or something was there in the void on the edge of the abyss. A purpose in eternity.

I prayed this prayer. Oh great Whale-reverse Jonah. Certainly the prayer of a fisherman—a big fish fisherman.

I was afraid Death was at my door.

Every night, before I fell asleep, I took my mind off the long-awaited knock, by watching the bobber float across the surface of the dark waters of my mind, until it winked under, out of sight, plunging on the bite of a big fish. Then and only then, could I let go, relax, close my eyes and drift off to sleep. The sight of the bobber going under always eased my passage into the darkness.

Why this worked, I don't know, but it did. Perhaps it was because it assured me that there was indeed something on the other end, on the other side, and though I could not see it, I felt it. I was fastened to it by that line, however slight, and while I slept it would hold me tight to this world, if only by ever so slender a thread.

This, I believe, is the reason why knots became such an obsession, for if I lost that fish I– lost my faith. In my state of mind, I thought if I lost the fish, my father might die—and everything else, my life, my family, would be lost forever as well. An irrational fear, yet strangely prophetic, in the mid-night hour.

Above all, one must be prepared, and knots are the key. The beginning and the end.

So I became an existential angler, one who fishes in the seas of life for significance and meaning, and I opened my eyes to the specific life-lessons, which fishing teaches, and which apply to every aspect of our lives: business and success, love and relationships, religion and faith. But most of all life and death.

I learned to dream big, to set specific goals and chase them down wherever they might lead even if it was one hundred miles out into the Gulf of Mexico, blue-water fishing, searching for an answer I could not find on shore.

For the sea, indefinite and infinite, is vast and wide, a stormy, unpredictable realm that will test your faith in ways undreamed of on the land.

Halloween, 2003: Gray clouds sweep across the sky. On the horizon the rain has already begun to fall slantwise, in dark, vertical sheets. The waves break and churn off the jetty, extending into the Gulf of Mexico at the southern tip of Pass-a-Grille, Florida. My father lies dying. Lymphoma and the aftermath of chemotherapy, have consumed him, ravaging his body, mind and spirit.

His liver is failing, he has diabetes and emphysema, as well as dementia, a condition of the mind, whereby his intellect has lost its bearings and he wanders lost amid empty, desolate rooms, calling out for his dead mother. The windows are always barred; the doors are locked. There is no escape.

He is in the room alone, with the exception of one other occupant - Death. It is searching him out he informs me.

He sees his dead mother there. I hear him talking to her. He's always cold and thirsty, on the verge of panic. Night after night, he calls out, asking me to come and save him, but I cannot. All I can do is to preside over his demise.

In addition to everything else, there were the weekly visits to the doctor, the daily chaos of Hospice nurses, checking his blood pressure, his blood sugar, the endless reams of paperwork (in triplicate), oxygen rentals, bed rentals, wheelchair rentals as well as the constant, ever-present threat of hurricanes, one after another, and what to do with an invalid in a wheelchair in the event of a catastrophic storm.

Despair, like the low, dark clouds overhead, had gathered on my horizon. Like the incessant hurricanes, which stalked the east and west coasts of Florida, the storms of life were still a ways off, but waiting to engulf and overwhelm me.

Yet it's difficult to be depressed in Florida, especially if you live on the beach; the balmy breezes, the blue skies, the perpetual sunshine, all paint Death's grotesque facade in bright clown make-up. I guess you might say I had a tropical depression.

2 Heart of a Champion: Lesson Of The Bonita

To take my mind off the nagging problems and to drive away the black funk of death and divorce, I did something simple and uncomplicated. I went fishing. For the first time in twenty-five years. Though I did not know it at the time, it was to become a tidal event in my life, which at its lowest, provided hope, and at its highest-joy.

I opened the door to the shed and took down an old fishing pole hanging overhead; the reel was fused to the rod with a thick coat of rust; the cork handle was half-eaten away, the guides, wires ready to crumble at a touch. The line, though still pliable, was brittle, a rusted hook and sinker at one end. The drag was tight and stiff, but with some oil and elbow grease, it loosened up considerably.

I dug a bobber out of an ancient tackle box, a few split-shots, a new hook and a bright orange stringer, in case I actually caught something. As I performed these simple tasks, a lightness of spirit swept through me, subtle as the wing of a butterfly. I could not yet tell exactly what it was, but I felt its presence—for an hour I was distracted, almost what you might call happy.

The very thought of fishing always brings a smile to my face and a happy flood of memories. Of fishing with my father as a boy on the sun-baked docks at Cedar Key, of spear-fishing in the Caribbean, while riding on my father's back, of standing with a cane pole, ankle deep in the semi-darkened creosote waters of Watermelon Pond, the tall proud oaks, overhung with Spanish moss, of fishing along the banks and lakes, the rivers and seas of my youth, the cloudless, eternal, untroubled blue skies of childhood overhead.

I was ready to try my luck. In truth I was looking to change it.

At first, I caught nothing but small insignificant fish, pinfish, and although they make an excellent bait; I did not yet know this, and quickly became frustrated. I would sit or stand and wait for hours just to catch small fish after small fish.

I quickly came to the realization that if this were fishing, I had neither the patience nor the inclination to continue. I was a teacher at a University, a writer, a divorced father of two, an educated man of the world. I had traveled extensively, all across the United States, Europe, the Middle East, North and South America; I had many duties and responsibilities to which to attend. I could not waste my time like this. I did not know it was only the first step on an existential journey—more of a leap than a step actually.

Although I used to love fishing with my father as a kid, as an adult, I was just too busy, too preoccupied with my career, which in truth, was going nowhere fast, and my family, which was now fractured beyond repair. I was casting about aimlessly, without purpose, catching nothing of any great significance either in life or in fishing.

In the end I did not quit, I dared not, for it was the only thing, which brought a ray of light into the darkness that had become my life. It was this expectation, which brought me, at the close of October, to the end of the jetty to fish.

I did not want to give up – I had no choice. It was my last chance to salvage something of the wreck of my life and find the courage to slog on.

I had a dream, however simple. To catch a big fish.

A royal flush in poker at the Bellagio in Las Vegas, a grand slam in the World Series, the Academy Award or a big fish on the end of your line – it all begins with a dream. But not just any dream – a big dream. Jonah's whale.

Above all it is a mindset, a strong-willed determination, for those who dare to dream big, that nothing less than the best will do. Far too many fishermen are content to sit on the rocks all day and fish for anything that bites.

They employ the same losing strategy and wonder why they continue to catch nothing but small fish day in day out. That was me; I used to be one of those fishermen. I would sit by the hour and fish. I caught some, lost some, it made little difference.

There was as yet no burning desire to do whatever it takes, to catch and land the big one, for catching is one thing, landing quite another. With luck you may catch your dream, it takes much more to land it and make a lasting dream come true. You will have to fight to the end—like the Bonita.

Once hooked, a big fish will almost always attempt one last desperate run, especially the great underrated game-fish known as the Bonita. One thing they all do: take one last run —always, even if you reel it in close to your boat, a bridge or a jetty, it will attempt one last desperate run, and it will keep doing it, until, on light tackle—it dies.

Every other fish quits: Snook fight furiously at first, but then they dog it; Barracuda will eventually tire and slow down; Tarpon become docile once they roll in exhaustion and show their belly. But the Bonita will fight forever.

I learned from the Bonita to be prepared for that last run—and fight on. I learned it one day when they struck in a school off the jetty out of the blue.

The sea, an unfathomable emerald green, sparkled with translucent clarity. I could see straight down through the water to the ripples in the sand on the bottom, made by the tide sweeping past.

A school of white bait, so profuse I could've walked across it, huddled close to the rocks on the tip of the jetty as a big school of Bonita shredded through their ranks. Whitebait is the best bait for Bonita.

It was cold-a mid-winter's day and the barometric pressure was falling fast; on the horizon the clouds were darkening to a deep blue-black, and the sky was beginning to crack open and drench us with a bitter cold rain. The lightning, though still a ways off, was, with each peal of thunder, unfurling the approaching storm. I could literally feel the hair on the back of my neck and arms standing up.

Loosely translated, Bonita means pretty or lovely or beautiful. Like a silver-blue projectile, its stream-lined body, adorned with curious, hieroglyphic motifs, whirls through the water like a dervish, hell-bent upon its Tran tic dance.

There were four other fisherman there that day.

"Look, I cried. "What a beautiful fish!"

One man, who sat hunched over near the trash can, pulled his rain-hood lower over his eyes and shrugged his shoulders. "a fish is a fish is a fish," he scoffed.

The unsighted see but do not see. Literal eyesight is what they use to get around without bumping into things. But to the sighted, there is an aesthetic value in the sight of a silver Bonita slashing through clean, bright blue-water. It is more than a fish.

That day, in early February, the Bonita were running in threes, roiling the waters as they hurtled through the bait schools, scattering them like leaves before the wind, as they ascended in an astonishing explosion at the surface, feeding on the run.

I could see them coming far down the beach, from fifty yards out, in pursuit of the bait, intertwining in an undersea arabesque, choreographed along the delicate edge of the blade of a knife- a flashing, slashing bolt of silver-blue, they rose as one, funneling the bait-fish into a V, before diving back down again, at half the speed of light, their prey locked in their powerful jaws.

Amid the sonic boom of thunder, the howling winds and slashing rain, they came on-again and again and again in a veritable frenzy. I hurled my cast net out into the bubbling cauldron of bait-fish. As I tried to hoist it back across the railing it was so heavy-laden I could barely lift it with both arms. When I finally opened it-the bait spilled out around my feet in an avalanche of quicksilver.

I baited my hook and cast out into the bubble. It did not take long. A jolt shot through my graphite fishing rod, straight up my arm to my elbow, nearly ripping my arm from its socket. I held on for dear life. Then—in a flash I had lost it or thought I had lost it. The line went slack, but it was merely running back towards me—a trick of the wily Bonita. Unpredictably in the fish's first blazing run as the rod bends double into your gut and your line snaps as taught as a violin string tuned to the highest pitch, the Bonita will often unexpectedly turn and head straight back towards you, throwing you off.

In that instant, while your line is slack, they will throw the hook and swim away. Whatever happens—keep your line taut.

A sharp retort of thunder overhead and things went from bad to worse. By the look of the blue-black bank of clouds on the horizon, I knew what was coming—a super cell. A bolt of lightning struck very close nearby, followed by a heart-rending crackling echo of thunder like the retort of a high-powered hunting rifle.

It echoed on, long after, unraveling the synapses along my already frayed nerve endings, tingling with an overdose of adrenalin. Out there on the jetty, I was cut off, exposed to the elements, with nowhere to hide.

Ironically, I noted that the jetty upon which I was standing, was surrounded by an iron railing, and that I held a graphite fishing rod in my hand, otherwise known as a lighting rod, not to mention the water all around, a super-conductor of electricity.

But I was not yet ready to call it a day. Too many fish in the water.

I watched as two other fishermen packed up their gear.

"That's it for me," shouted one, as he crawled away like a miserable cur with its tail between its legs.

"It's not worth dying for," agreed the other, sprinting toward the street through the pouring rain.

Ha!" I never felt so alive. My heart rate had more than doubled, I was shivering with cold, my hands trembled, my teeth chattered, I was drenched to my second skin, but I would have caught the lightning in my teeth and spit it out for the chance to catch a Bonita. I was all in.

"I don't give a damn if I do get struck by lighting!" Said the fisherman over by the trash can. Trash-Can Man threw back his hood and laughed out loud, and as it rang with the sound of the thunder, I detected a crazy something in his eyes.

A little spark of madness there. "Either it will give me supernatural powers or kill me," he laughed. "Either way is fine with me."

We watched the advance of the super-cell.

"Fish on!" Shouted Trash-Can Man, his voice hoarse and harsh from the wind and the rain. He fought a Bonita down the wet, slippery rocks to a little beach to the south. It took him out in the water up to his waist—with lightning striking all around, but he fished on.

I thought he was really crazy until I got a strike-and had to fight my own Bonita down the rocks, the rain stinging my eyes, as I fought for footing, to the little sandy beach and out into the water almost up to my shoulders. It was still running out to sea at an unstoppable pace. I knew if I battened down my drag I would lose it. But I could not stay in the water like this with lighting all around. What could I do? I fished on.

Then it did something Bonita will often do. One last trick – one final surprise. It ran straight back toward me—at me in fact. Be prepared for this when fishing for Bonita. I can't say it enough: Keep your line taut at all times.

Trash-Can Man landed the Bonita, hauled it back up to the jetty and cut its throat to bleed it out; it thrashed and beat about for another ten to fifteen minutes, its severed juggler spewing blood like a fire hydrant.

I fought my Bonita in close to the shore, and thought I had it landed-when suddenly it slashed back out as strong and as fast as it had at first and snapped my line.

I was not prepared for the ferocious tug, so I lost it. That made two I had lost. But I was not ready to quit. Not yet. Maybe not ever!

I raced back up to the jetty.

The clouds were racing towards us now, perceptibly darker, pitch black and ominous, back-lit from within by intermittent flashes of lightning, so close overhead they pressed down claustrophobically low, the cold rain falling harder now, sleeting slantwise with the wind. I could barely make out the knot I was trying to tie to the hook.

One thing, however, I did see was Bonita, by the hundreds. The feeding frenzy was definitely on as the bottom dropped out of the barometer.

I watched a lightning bolt hit the water twenty yards away, forked fingers flashing under the green water just as it flashes across the sky. The water bubbled and smoked. When I touched the iron railing encircling the jetty it was hot.

"Shit!" cursed Garbage-Can Man. "That's it for me." He pulled the hood back over his face, snapped his tackle-box shut and slung his gear and the Bonita across his shoulder.

That left me. Who was the crazy one here? Even the Garbage-Can Man was making an exit. But he had already caught one. I wanted to go—I really did, desired with all my heart to go home. Have a hot cocoa with those little marshmallows.

I have two children. I live in the lightning capital of the world. The following day I read in the St. Petersburg Times, that a female tourist and her son had been struck by lightning; it had killed the boy and put her into a coma. I talked to the doctor who operated on her. Her spleen had been blackened, he said-cooked.

As I said, I wanted to go, in fact, my mind insisted I go, but my fingers kept tying that knot as if they had a life of their own.

I cast out again—again a Bonita struck—this time there was no stopping it, so I fought on, the line un-spooling to the end of my spool.

I reeled back in some line, getting it close to the jetty, it ran back out again, fresh as ever. I reeled it in, it ran back out. This went on until I was ready to dog it.

And then, the weather, fickle as ever, changed. The day spun, half gray, half blue in an atmospheric anomaly. A thick fog began to roll in, casting the outlines of the dunes and sea-oats in a shroud of shadows, gilding the emerald seas-surreal.

Cut off out there at the end of the jetty, alone, fog-bound, it felt like I was lost at sea; I half expected to see the Flying Dutchman to come sailing out of the mists.

And still I fished on hooked to lightning of different sort—a bolt-of silver blue. It had granted me supernatural powers after all- the power to see something through to the end, to fight on, to never give up, to endure till the end of time if I must.

It took a long, long time, but I finally got the fish in close enough to observe the mysterious hieroglyphic designs on its sides, and in the enigma of those empiric configurations, written in fire on the flanks of a fish, I was granted a vision of sorts, however fleetingly—through the dark green waters of the storm--what the Greeks call Anagnorisis, a critical insight into life, yet an insight which occurs too late because the tragedy is already set in motion. Up ahead aways, but the train has already left the tracks.

The fish spun and raced back out. Nothing could stop this fish—as nothing could stop my destiny from unfolding-it was already laid out in front of me, and I could not change what lay ahead.

It ran on forever.

I learned through bitter experience, that it is here, upon the landing of a big Bonita, that most fishermen lose their fish, most people, their dream.

The unexpected throws us off, and we lose our balance. In an instant what we thought was a sure thing becomes another lost opportunity and disappointment inevitably sets in. Here we lose heart. Sometimes the cost of victory is too high.

Count on it- there will always be one last problem, one final difficulty, one ultimate conundrum, just as all your dreams are about to come true, which if not anticipated and corrected, will snatch your dream right out from under your nose, in the very act of consummation, making the loss, all the more heart-breaking.

At this point many give up.

Yet the quality of water is buoyancy. It will keep your dream afloat. If fishing has taught me anything it is to never give up; to sustain that buoyancy.

There is always one last chance, one last cast. It is an existential lesson, which only experience and loss upon loss can teach. The alternate meaning of the term, "fish on," meaning an angler has a fish on his line and other anglers should get out of his way, is to keep going in times of adversity, to never give up – to remain buoyant. To fish on-

In the beginning as I fished the rocks on the jetty, rain or shine, for whatever might be biting I was lured into that futile endeavor with signs of hope, for every once in a while my bobber would plunge and I would catch my breath –maybe this time…

But these were false signs: in the end, my line almost always re-surfaced on an empty hook, the bait stolen or worse, stuck on the rocks. Countless times I lost my entire rig to small fish: hook, line and sinker.

The cost, however, accrued to more than financial loss: it was an expense in time and energy. I felt used. Many times I almost gave up. Then one day the tides turned and I learned a valuable lesson.

At the change of certain tides, out of sight, just below the waterline, visible only at low tide, I observed the rocks were strewn with the spindrift of snagged and tangled lines, shredded cast nets, lost lures and many a broken dream..

Whether it is a business partnership, a friendship or a marriage, do not waste your time and energy with the half-hearted attempt of people who do not or will not give you their all. In the end it will come to nothing. You have to fight for what you believe in.

For a time I settled for the little fish, and they taught me well. I learned to differentiate the bite: little fish nibble.

They nibble at your bait and nibble away at your dreams until little by little until there's nothing left. All your time, energy and passion—it comes to nothing. That is the dead giveaway.

Big fish- like the Bonita bite, and they bite hard. They give it their all—everything. They commit. All in, win, lose or draw. And there will be a fight- make no bones about it. When you are dreaming of the big one, you too must commit, give it your all, never give up, because the big fish leaves you not with a sense of loss or regret, but of inspiration and the motivation to fish on. For you have felt in its transformational pull, the power of a big dream, and on the turn of the next tide, you know you will try again, and perhaps next time…

Never give up. That is the lesson of the Bonita.

When the fight with the Bonita was over that day, I was tired, hungry, wet, cold and miserable. I caught a terrible cold, as well as bronchitis, which lasted well over a week. My only victory lay in the fact that I did not quit. I had given it my all. So we fish on and fight on, beating against the tides of chance and circumstance, hearts buoyant with hope until, like the Bonita, we win or die trying.

Heart of a champion.

3 Dreaming Of The Big One: Lesson Of The Snook

The Tampa Bay area, Clearwater, Tampa, St. Petersburg and Sarasota, with its winding waterways, mangrove islands, sheltered flats and beaches, is one hell of a place to practice the art and craft of fishing. I am a fisher of dreams, and running through all my dreams is the big golden one – the Linesider, also known as the Nightstalker, or Robolo, a great golden fish, with a long black lateral stripe along its back— Florida's great game fish, the Snook.

During Snook season if you can catch a Snook, you can keep it, but first you have to catch it – it's like catching a dream. Should you be lucky enough to catch the turn of the tide in your favor, take note of the time and place in your fisherman's journal, for of all fish, Snook seem to run on Swiss movements. If you forget everything else about Snook, this is the thing to remember. Return the next day, same place and time- to the hour and the minute, and it will bite once more. But you must return again and again and again. It takes practice to go up against the best.

In winter, Snook like to sun themselves in the shallow cuts adjacent to the mangrove islands. Look for a tidal swash, where water surges through a channel and flows into the deeper flats toward the sea.

Toss a free-lined select shrimp or pinfish under the mangrove banks and let it drift with the current, or bounce a jig slowly across the bottom to entice this most elusive of prey. On clear days, try walking the dog with a top-water, on over-cast days, a diver. Cast to every corner of the flats, trying every level of the water column. Find the fish.

I have spent hours at this, waiting for the turn of the tide. And that is another lesson-patience. Sometimes you have to wait for your dream to come true, but the tide will turn, and you will find fish if they are there.

A high, outgoing tide is best, up under the mangroves, around an oyster bar, the water moving.

I recommend a stout braided line with a 36-45 inch Stren Tinted fluorocarbon leader, (the tint takes even the sparkle from the sun out of the line) and is invisible underwater to the Snook's sharp eyes; add a light wire #2 semi-circle Mustad hook for the most natural presentation. Get rid of all hardware. Above all avoid snaps or swivels, bobbers and split shots whenever possible. Keep it simple. Tie a line to line knot, from your braid to your fluorocarbon leader. This will increase your odds of catching this hard-fighting game fish.

I did not know all this at the time I caught and lost my first big one. It was pure chance, fisherman's luck. On that chilly, overcast October day, one last cast, and I decided to head home, a phrase, which ever-afterwards, was to become enshrined as a familiar refrain. When my children hear me say this, they roll their eyes. "One last Cast," what it really means is until I catch a fish. It could be one cast or one hundred.

My little red and white bobber dipped and swirled in the dancing eddies at the western tip of the jetty.

Abruptly and, without warning--the bobber disappeared beneath the water, as if it had never been there at all- and the drag began to sing. Something big was on the other end. Something unexpectedly powerful, and if I could've read the signs -exceptionally meaningful.

Never had I felt anything like it! It hit with a jolt so sudden it nearly yanked me into the water. At 6'1, 205 pounds, my feet actually slid across the rocks.

I had to set myself to keep from being pulled in. Brace yourself. Brace for it because when you dream big – you need to be grounded if it is to become more than a dream. Though your head in the clouds, your feet must touch the earth. As in any sport, there are practical rules to fishing.

I tried to halt the big fish's run, by lifting the rod tip and hauling back with all my might, but watched in awe, unable to stop it, as the reel ratcheted into a long mechanical wail, the line running out with a power that was impossible to check. The jolt sent me reeling back on my heels, the muscles in my arms tensing for a fight.

My rod bent double under its sheer weight. I loosened the drag, so the line would not snap and let him run. There was no stopping him anyway.

This was fun! Ha!

He ran all right. I steadied myself, and tried to remain calm, to master myself as well as the fish. The line whipped sideways through the white-caps, slanting with the fish's run. The line tightened then the fish turned. Ran in a completely opposite direction toward shore. And I ran with it, down the rocks.

The line was taut, ready to snap, a Stradivarius tuned to its highest pitch. I pulled up, the fish was rising too, finally coming up.

Up it came, out of the water, long and golden, flashing in the last rays of the setting sun. A giant Linesider- at least 44 inches long, 20-25 pounds, it seemed to jump forever.

A long black lateral line swept along the curvature of its spine toward a powerful, grille-plate, jutting into a lethal predator's jaw, which can best be described as prehistoric.

I clambered further down the rocks, fighting it in one last, desperate surge. The salt-spray made the rocks slippery, and I clung to the rod with both hands, like a tennis pro smashing a back-hand, not even bothering to reel anymore. I had to watch my step or I would fall, so I concentrated on keeping the fish on the line somehow. It was a fast dash across those slippery rocks, and I was afraid of falling and bashing my brains out, but I kept my feet somehow. I did not even have time to look where I was stepping.

Then the line went slack – dead, and something snapped like a whip-lash.

As I reeled back hard—too hard, my knot, the weakest link in any fisherman's repertoire- broke, leaving my line luffing in the breeze, a curlicue of unraveled thread at one end. The tell-tell sign of knot breakage. I pressed my face against the rocks, bowed down before the fates. I did not care who saw me.

That night I went home, fell on my knees and wept. When it had counted most my knot had failed. It had not held my hopes or dreams; now it was all slipping away: career and family, my father, dying. Lost. All seemed inextricably bound up together. Lose one, lose them all.

When I got up from my knees, I summoned my courage. I gazed with new eyes at the situation, with a fisherman's eyes. I had after all hooked a big one.

It may have gotten away, but if I learned to tie a knot that could hold I might land it yet. I would not give up; I would fish on.

Lesson three: In life as in fishing, everything comes back to the basics: It all begins and ends with a knot. In such a way, do small issues lead on to larger ones; For knots are essential to our lives: with it, a surgeon secures an artery and saves a life; with a square knot the sailor circumnavigates the globe; our shoelaces, before the introduction of Velcro, are usually our first introduction to the intricacy of knots, and are the knots from which all others are measured.

If we don't get that first knot right, we will lack the confidence to walk, then run; we will trip all over ourselves the rest of our lives. To learn to tie a good, strong knot, one that holds fast, requires patience, practice and discipline, virtues which fishing teaches.

I was using 10 pound mono-filament line on my rig, with a small J hook, and that fish ran it all the way off the spool and snapped it like a thread, yet it was not in the strength of the line, nor the size of the hook, nor even the knot itself, for large fish have been caught by master fishermen on light line and hook, it was in the character of the fisherman who had tied the knot.

It was simple: I was not yet ready—not prepared for the big one.

I had tied a simple, overhand knot, the only one I knew and remembered, and it had not held when the big fish came. That was all. It was a lesson I would take to heart, but not right away, because I did not want to exert the extra effort to learn just yet.

Furthermore, I had hooked a late-season Linesider. A fighter, second only to the Tarpon, prized by anglers throughout the state, and I had almost pulled it off.

Although I lost the fish, I had caught something infinitely more important: The ability to dream again --a big dream. With that fish, the storm had broken. I felt alive again for the first time in a long time. I also had a goal. A dream of the big one. A Snook.

A lengthy divorce had robbed me of the dream of a family and almost broken my spirit. My career as a writer was stalled.

A bitter betrayal at work had sapped my faith in my fellow man, and with my father in the throes of death, I was lonely, frustrated, bitterly unhappy.

Yet something about the way that big fish had hit and then fought had given me something to believe in again.

It was more than a dream-- more than a fish; It awakened in me a desire—though I was down I wanted to get back up and make my dream come true. All was not lost if I did not give up. I felt like a champion. God- the universe, fate had sent me a dream to strive for, to believe in, to make my own. I told death to take a hike—I was going fishing.

In my darkest hours the thought comforted me.

Once a friend and I constructed a little wooden vessel from discarded scraps of plywood, stolen from a construction site around the neighborhood. We sawed the wood and sanded it down, then fitted the sides together to form the bow, turned it over and hammered and drove the nails into the planking to secure the bottom. We even painted a name, which I cannot remember, on the side of our little wooden vessel.

We carried it down to Hogtown Creek, in Gainesville, Florida and set sail. It actually floated. All summer long we sailed it down the winding creeks, which rose on the heavy rains of summer, armed with a cane pole and a tin can full of earthworms dug from the rich black earth, which lined the banks. We caught hundreds of Sunnys, small sunfish in the fishing holes.

My black lab, Blackie rode in the bow, nose to the wind. I remember the feeling of wanting to be there, doing that above all else forever. Fishing on water.

That feeling had returned. The sun had come out. The storm had passed. I was going to learn how to fish, and this time I would catch the big fish, and by good fortune, happy accident, chance--destiny or stroke of fate, I lived right beside the best fishing hole in the world. A block to the east, was Boca Ciega Bay, the Pass at Pass-a-Grille to the south; to the west, my front yard was the Gulf of Mexico, plunging to depths of 90 feet, off Eggmont Key, a nearby island. I could almost cast to there from the jetty.

I was a happy man, but more than that-I was lucky.

I had been lucky—yes, but it was beginner's luck. Now I had to muster the skill required to master this new calling, but I also would have to learn to understand the tides and waters in which I lived. I was determined to hook, to fight and most of all to land a large Snook. To experience that adrenalin rush again, to feel that up-lifting force once more, to overrule Thanatos, the death-wish. To take my life back.

To make that dream come true and fulfill my desires would take hard work; first I would have to re-learn everything I thought I knew, for if I didn't even understand the elementary basics of knot tying, what kind of fisherman could I hope to be?

That night before I dozed off my eyes were filled with the sight of that red and white bobber going under. I never slept better, and awoke the next morning ready to begin my new life as a fisherman. It would take me trout fishing on the flats of Fort Desoto, to the Crystal River in Colorado; shark-fishing in the Gulf, kayak fishing for Tarpon in the Keys; and 100 miles out, blue-water fishing for Marlin. Along the way I would become a better fisherman and a better man; and I would learn to trust the turn of the tide. It was a portent of things to come, but first I had to learn to tie a little knot. A knot to bind a big fish, a knot to hold a dream.

4 Take Your Kids Fishing On A Star

There are few pleasures more fulfilling than fishing with your father. For me, the best part is spending the entire day together. In the thrilling semi-darkness of early dawn, we'd set out for parts unknown, with a sense of impending adventure and the feeling that anything was possible. I always hoped I'd catch a big one that day—one to make my father proud. I'd dream about it all night, yet I could never quite figure out what is was that kept me awake, restlessly tossing and turning. That ever-elusive something just out of reach, which we sometimes long for all our lives, yet are never quite able to attain.

Looking back, it was my father who was out of reach.

Usually I caught rather small, insignificant fish, nothing to brag on, but one day, on my 7th birthday, along the sun-baked docks at Cedar Key, I hooked and landed a large speckled trout. It was the biggest fish I'd ever caught, and the one I will always remember most. It swims through my memory, flashing like silver in the blue crest of a breaking wave.

Three photographic images hang on my wall, resting under glass. All are black and white. One is of me that day, holding my catch up to show my father, the next, taken with an old Brownie Camera, is of my father as a boy fishing from a bridge in New Jersey, and captures him holding up his catch to his father; the third, of my own son, shows him with a large Snook he caught in the summer of 2006 off the seawall in Pass-a-Grille.

He too holds up his fish to me, his own father. Each of us, from father to son, across the span of three generations, stands there, our fish in our hands, holding our trophy up to the appraising eyes of our fathers.

As I walked by the photos one day, something I've done a thousand times before, I was struck by the expression on our faces. Each of us is smiling-that same mysterious smile, as if we'd uncovered the secret of life.

It got me thinking. What is it about fishing with our fathers that we seem to hold in such high regard? Even long after the days of our youth. It's a simple act. I've asked around, queried other fisherman, and the feeling is universal. Of having and holding our father's complete attention, however momentarily, an awareness that as such an important part of our lives, the parent, usually so elusive and out of reach, has suddenly and unexpectedly become accessible—and we are bonded with him, and know him as if for the first time. For many, fishing seems to be that bond. With baseball, there are too many distractions for our father's attention; with fishing it is just you and him.

Furthermore, it is a sweet time out of time, when we are in this world as innocents, before Stealth Bombers and foreign wars, before marriage and children, before college, friends and careers whisk us away from our fathers forever, before we realize what we have lost.

It was to me, to paraphrase a familiar Disney tune, like fishing on a star.

For on that day all my dreams came true, and I found myself in a long line of succession, flowing backwards through time, fishing in a river of fathers and sons.

My father's father, Harry Golden, was a famous author, and to hear my father tell it, his father was a very busy man. He was in fact, away much of the time.

Yet, from the photo, he made time to take my father fishing, and that is what is remembered most. Harry was a best-selling author and newspaper editor extraordinaire.

During the 1950's Harry wrote 21 bestselling books, including the biggest of them all in the 50's-Only In America, an ubiquitous phrase that has since entered into the cultural lexicon of our time.

In the late 50's Harry owned and operated his own newspaper, The Carolina Israelite, which included subscribers from all over the United States, including two Nobel Prize winners: Ernest Hemmingway (again-the connection to Hemmingway) and William Faulkner, as well as John Steinbeck, and poets, Robert Frost and Carl Sandburg.

In his rambling two story house off Elizabeth Avenue in Charlotte, North Carolina, a classic letter from Albert Einstein rested under glass. Harry wrote the renowned scientist, asking him to explain the Theory of Relativity for his reader. Einstein's reply:" Come up to Princeton and I'll play if for you on the violin."

But it was his newspaper he loved best. As I rambled through his old house I was struck by the printing press. Today at the click of a mouse, the computer performs layout and design for the editor. Type and font are set automatically, but Harry had a typesetter in his employ.

In those days typesetting was an art. A good typesetter had to set type in what was then colorfully referred to as a slug-line, the placement of individual letters of the alphabet upside down and backwards in mirror-image, one letter at a time to correctly anticipate what the page would look like when it came rolling off the presses. (The articles **an** and **the** came out in one solid unit, and were therefore, easier to set.)

But it was the power of words to effect change of which he was most proud. When the KKK allegedly burned his newspaper to the ground for his stand on civil rights, he rebuilt. And the next headline proclaimed for one and all to see: "Ideas don't burn."

As I look at the photos of my father with his fish, time skips a beat, and I'm back again, in Harry's old house: the cigar store Indian on the front porch, the books, which line the shelves, the photos of the famous and not so famous, the man himself, rocking in his old wooden rocker, a glass of bourbon and soda in one hand, a good cigar in the other, and I'm reminded of what really counts—our connection to the past, the customs and traditions which keep us together as a family, a nation or a country, and I know my father's father took time to take him fishing. I see it in the photograph. In the timeless smile.

My father was the one who taught me to fish. An honest man, he worked for thirty years as a Professor at the University of Florida, lectured around the country as an Edgar Allan Poe scholar and wrote several books, the last, his autobiography on his deathbed. He too was a busy man, a man of letters and affairs, yet he too took the time to take a little boy out fishing, to teach him to tie a knot and bait his hook, to cast out and catch a big fish. He had his own life, but he stopped the world for me. You can see it in the photo. In my smile.

Now as I return the favor to my own son, I realize although our world moves at a speed unheard of when I was growing up, when Sky and I are fishing together, time waits at our command. For father and son are fishing you see, and nothing can come between us. It is our time together.

We follow where the day leads, at ease beneath the sun, wandering at our will, and so long as our hearts beat, not to the hands of a clock, but to the eternal vagaries of timelessness, infinite as space, the world is ours.

Here I fish uncharted waters; there are no channel markers to guide me. It is a realm of bottomless depths, the relationship between father and son, deep and vast and wide as the sea. It is a far other fish I seek today, not one caught on hook and leader, but one which swims through the past, forever out of reach. The love of my father.

In the end I do not know what it is about fishing with our fathers. I only know my father cared enough to take me fishing. Maybe that's why we're all smiling in the photos. Not because we caught a fish; or a star, no -because we caught our father.

And so we reach out for our dreams, and that star, which has always eluded us, shines a little brighter, if only in our memory, on the sun-baked docks at Cedar Key, from a bridge in New Jersey, or surf-fishing from the shore, we are there once more, fishing with our fathers, in that never-ending dawn of infinite possibility.

And so the rod bends double, the line snaps taught and the drag sings sweetly as in a dream. The memory remains. Of my father and of my father's father—of my son, and one day, his son. And beyond that, to all my fathers, back through time to the first fisherman, the father of us all.

Fishing on a star. And fathers with their daughters, of course.

5 On The Rocks: Lesson Of The Lowly Pinfish

Sometimes the answer is right there in front of you. So it was with the pin-fish.

It took three years of patience and hard-won discipline to learn the lessons required to hook and land a big game-fish like the Snook, but first I had to catch a lot of little fish, starting with the pin-fish, ironically, the Snook's favorite food.

Each species is inter-related. The more you learn about one species, the easier the others are to understand. A Spanish Mackerel, for instance, swims low in the water column, so the successful fisherman must know what kind of bait also swims low, or if using a lure or a silver spoon, must use an egg-sinker to keep the spoon low; Redfish best like to feed near oyster bars on the flats, on the incoming and outgoing tides, so you learn all there is to know about oyster beds; trout consume different baits at different times of the day, year, and phases of the moon, so you have to know what's in the water to "match the hatch," as they say.

I learned the lessons well. I paid attention to the old salts around the bridges and jettys and docks; I kept an inshore journal, in which I faithfully recorded species caught, baits and times, so I could use this information later, when I was ready. I had always had good luck-I knew this with certainty—but I wanted the skill to match.

It all began with that Snook off the jetty, one of the most difficult and demanding of fish to catch, for they are shy and secretive and do not give up their mysteries easily.

You must stalk them where they live, learn to think like they do. Timing is of the essence. Of utmost importance, is time of day and tides.

Look for moving water—the faster the better, as an apex predator, Snook like to lay in wait amid the mangroves or under bridges and near jetties to ambush prey; its eyesight, like that of an eagle's, is exceptional. In clear water, therefore, you must become a Snook to catch a Snook. A Snook Whisperer as it were.

I learned to wade up-current, so that when I presented my bait, it flowed naturally, drifting down-current on an outgoing tide at a particular hour of the day or night, which may mean the difference between success and failure, for if you are there at the wrong time, the Snook will ignore your offering; although you may view hundreds of Snook stacked up right under your nose, they will remain tantalizingly out of reach. Arrive at the right time, however, and it will be vastly different, and you may miss it by minutes. You may give up and move on, just as the Snook begin to bite.

It is up to you to discover the exact time, and specific hour, early morning or late afternoon, to the minute when the Snook bite is on; if you do you will catch as many as you can as fast as you can reel them in. I once caught 26 in a row. They will not stop biting until the pre-determined hour when the bite mysteriously ceases as suddenly as it began.

Bring your watch and check it often. As the minutes tick down a lump will catch in your throat as your heartbeat quickens because you know what's coming. Expect it! It will happen. Time and time again this has proven true. They work on Swiss movements.

Furthermore, Snook are finicky eaters, preferring one bait over another at odd times; one day they will inhale a live shrimp with a vengeance, and the next, utterly ignore it, preferring a Spanish Sardine or a thread-fin instead. It's all in the tides and the seasons.

It's up to you, the fisherman, to be prepared to compensate, to discover the right bait on the spot, using a cast net, expertly thrown, to "match the hatch" or a top-water lure, or bottom-bouncing jig-- whatever is in the water and being eaten at the time. That's all there is to it.

Ha!

Sometimes a plug or lure will capture a Snook's attention, yet more often than not, they will only follow it in, then idly swim away, so it's best to have a reserve of live bait on hand. I tie a bait bucket to my belt when I'm wading the flats, so I'm ready. A white buck-tail jig with a red head works well, so does a top-water plug.

I was using a red and white bomber one day, "walking the dog" (twitching the rod-rip in a back and forth motion to make the lure walk on water) when a big Snook followed it all the way to where I stood up to my knees on the flats; my heart skipped a beat as he rose out of the water right under me. But he didn't touch it. Once, off the jetty, in gin-clear waters, I netted a finger-mullet and tossed it in on the end of my hook. A large Snook, maybe 45 inches (at first I thought it was a small Tarpon), rose up from the depths and hit the small mullet. He ran with it in his mouth. Everyone was looking on in awe-some yelling set the hook, others, shouting in disbelief, how big it was. I took a breath and tried to count to ten, but only got to three before I tried prematurely to set the hook and it ate half my bait and got away. Snook are smart.

Slash and burn does not work with these maddening, unpredictable, noble and beautiful fish; it requires patience, disciple and hard-honed skills to first catch then land one. When using larger live bait, it pays to count to seven (at least) to allow the Snook to inhale the bait and the hook. Hard to do, but it pays off.

Furthermore, many fisherman, myself included, have hooked a Snook, only to lose it during the fight, usually at the moment when it leaps from the water into the air, so the attentive fisherman must always be on guard, watching his line play out, setting the hook, prepared to lean your rod out forward as it rises, at the appropriate time when it makes its jump in an effort to throw the hook.

I don't know how they do it, but I've lost so many Snook, when I was sure I had them hooked-when I had fought them for a minute or so with the hook set in their jaw, only to lose them at the last moment, my hook flying back empty.

If you're off a fraction of a second, you'll lose it. Watch your line, as it strains taut with the weight of the big fish; at the moment it straightens out completely—wait before you set the hook. Take a deep breath. Count to seven. Let the adrenalin surge. Then, with a flick of the wrist, set hook. If you miss it will suddenly snap slack, and wheel back, whipping past your head, leaving you wondering how the fish does it. Snook are not like other fish. It takes a sure touch. The unprepared and uninitiated will lose it every time.

That is Snook fishing.

All this you must accomplish during the hottest most sweltering months of summer, July and August in Florida, when the very asphalt beneath your feet melts in the parking lot on your way to the mangroves at the north end of Fort Desoto.

As you wade into the backcountry, between the cuts, where the big Snook congregate, dark clouds of mosquitoes swarm around your face, and the sudden showers and thunderstorms of summer roll in, unfurling flashes of lightning, while you stand hip-deep in the water with a lightning rod in one hand, the sweat pouring down your face and into your eyes as you coax your fingers around another complex knot, so you can tie another hook and leader on, which you just lost to a big Snook on the fly, as it torpedoed back under the mangroves and sliced your thirty pound test like thread, and the adrenalin pumps so fast your fingers fumble with the knot like a blind man tolling the rosary; yet in your excitement you can't wait to see if your knot slips tight, effortlessly against the eye of the hook or if not, watch the loops become tangled, and you start all over again.

Once luck is ruled out, and it's skill that counts, it's difficult. It really is.

If you don't execute your timing just right, your big fish will swim away, while the shrimp in your hand is snapping back and forth, and it stings you with its tail, drawing blood, meanwhile you're losing precious time because the Snook, you can count on it, will stop biting at any moment. This is always in the back of your mind, because just as suddenly as the bite begins-- it ends, and it's over. Time to call it a day and count up the won and lost ledger.

I tell you this only because the beginner does not know all this; he only knows he wants to catch another Snook—bad! I had fallen in love with fishing, now I had to find a way to consummate my desire. It was a great challenge, but the obsession became so great, that later, when in its throes, I would rather fish, than eat, drink or sleep.

The best fisherman, I have noticed, the most successful ones, seem to be running away from something, some inner grief or hurt, some secret torment, and so are absorbed in this sport where you are pitted against nature itself and the character of your own nature, good and bad.

For years I caught no great Snook; I only caught the lowly pinfish, and it almost drove me mad. To be so close to my dream- yet incapable of making it a reality was frustrating. But I was dogged and determined.

I also determined not to let my father die without a fight. I would challenge the biggest fish of all—death itself.

I got him up and walking around the room with a walker. I can see him still, shuffling along, his spindly legs, his swollen, purple ankles—one step at a time, taking his last steps toward oblivion.

It was painful to watch the once proud and vibrant man who, in his time had been a renowned Poe Scholar and author on F. Scott Fitzgerald, a globe-trotting Professor, teaching in Buenos Aires, Argentina on a Fullbright Scholarship, and in San Juan, Puerto Rico, in Ohio, New Orleans, and the University of Florida, who graduated from Kenyon College, Tulane and Columbia University in New York with a Ph.D.

In the beginning he could only take a step or two before he had to sit down and rest, wheezing like an old man on verge of a heart attack.

Still he walked on, as I fished on, both of us in it to the end.

One day he said, "I walked seven steps today." It seemed small and insignificant, yet it was a momentous stride forward.

"Next," he smiled, "I'll be dancing the Pass-e-Doble!"

Each of us, in our own way, was taking our first steps toward something new, neither of us backing down from the fight of our lives.

This was war--death up close and personal. The ever-present shadow. Perhaps that is why we cast a shadow, to remind us of the looming presence of the Dark One at our side.

That first year, however, found me utterly unprepared for the challenge. While my father took his first steps, I sat on the edge of the rocks at the end of the jetty and caught nothing but pinfish.

All I could do was dream of the big one, for unknown to me the Snook had moved on, migrating to warmer waters among the mangroves and down the winding rivers, which dot the state. I did not yet fully understand the migratory habits of Snook, nor the stubborn pride of dying fathers.

All I had in the beginning was hope. I hoped to catch another big fish, and land it this time, but nothing happened, and I came to learn another important lesson – hope is not enough to make your dreams come true. I had to grow, to adapt, to evolve into a fisherman with an understanding of my quarry and a successful strategy to catch it. Yet each failure brought a small success.

I learned to fail, to know what did not work, so I was forced to devise another strategy, something new, something to bring me closer to success, because I was never going to catch anything in life or in fishing if I didn't change. Failure is in itself, a revelation.

To make matters worse, periodically, the small fish would steal my bait and run me down into the rocks. My hook would snag and I would lose my line and my leader, but that was about it.

This also occurred in my writing career. I had optioned a few screenplays, made a little money here and there, but ultimately—nothing big. Just a lot of empty promises, from people pretending to be big fish, who were only little fish, dragging me down into the rocks, in the end stealing my time and energy. Beware the little fish.

In the end I was stuck, and gradually, little by little, the dream receded, leaving me empty-handed and ready to quit.

I was on the rocks.

Constantly forced to replace my line, tie another leader on, form another knot, bite another split-shot, add a bobber, a hook and shrimp, I learned something vitally important: failure, something everyone must go through before they succeed. Failure taught me how to wait it out, to sit through the slack tides; to remain grounded as the seasons and the tides changed. It also taught me what I did not want- small fish.

One of the things I learned was how to differentiate the touch of a fish at the other end of the line, weather big or small, weather a waste of my time or worth pursuing; for many things are just that- a waste of time. Failure teaches you to separate the two.

I practiced my timing as well--to set the hook so a fish stayed hooked.

This is particularly true in Tarpon fishing, where you must set the hook repeatedly as it makes its run—violently even—yanking back hard time and again and again, because a Tarpon's jaw is tough cartilage and the point of the hook must be driven in deep.

With other fish all that is required is a nimble touch, a flick of the wrist when you feel the bite. I learned the hard way, and lost a lot of fish in the process, but I learned.

As if to lure me on in this exercise in futility, every once in a while the bobber would plunge beneath the surface, and hope would return with the promise of a big fish fulfilled, yet, to further dash my expectations, it re-surfaced with an empty hook, the bait stolen or worse, stuck on the rocks again.

This was to be my second lesson of the lowly pin-fish. The promise of the big dream, without the substance, leads to disappointment and often surrender.

For of all things, which make life worth living, a dream is central to our existence, and if deferred for too long, can lead to ruin. You lose heart on the rocks, catching nothing but pin-fish and eventually you give up.

I am here to tell you—don't. Adapt, evolve, change, but keep going…

Too many people have tried and failed to catch and land their big dream, have fought a few battles, maybe won a few fights, but after repeated failures, they give up because the big dream continues to elude them. They are on the rocks, and the rocks are crisscrossed with the cast-off tackle of big dreamers: tattered cast nets, lost lures, twisted hooks and broken line. The one that got away.

The secret I learned the hard way was that change is necessary to land a dream. No one starts out a winner, you must learn as you go. If you are not winning, adapt, change. Sometimes you do have to try something completely different, pursuing your dream in other ways, in a new direction. Sometimes a dream has to be caught indirectly. Sometimes little things – like the pin-fish, lead on to bigger dreams.

The key is to remain undefeated, ready to try again, to re-tie any knot, re-bait any hook, to wait patiently for the change of the tide, for it will change, and that small change, sometimes seemingly insignificant, will often lead on to success.

I had to catch lots of pin-fish before I caught a Snook. Yet little did I realize I had the very thing I needed in my hands all along.

Learn about one species to learn about another.

The way which finally worked for me was to literally get up and move- to change to a different location because the big fish weren't biting where I was fishing, not the ones I wanted. Something which was not easy to do, because the dream – the giant Snook- had first appeared to me at the end of the jetty.

To me that spot was magic. I could not imagine recapturing it anywhere else; I would have waited there forever for it to return –only it didn't.

Worse, I began to sense it wasn't going to. There were only pin-fish there now. The timing was not right, the big fish had moved on, and so I had to move with them if I wanted to follow my dream.

It did not seem right at first. I was reluctant. It felt like giving up. I was comfortable in my spot.

My favorite fishing spot, down among the rocks at the end of the jetty where the big dream of the Snook had first made it presence known. There was no better place on earth. The water was deep and pure and clear, the sunsets breathtaking, and it was right across the street from my house. Convenience is often the enemy of achievement.

Other nagging frustrations intervened to halt my forward momentum, which at the time did not seem advantageous, yet in hindsight, were designed to get me up off my butt and go in search of my dream: it seemed the universe was in alignment against me.

As soon as I wanted to go fishing it would begin to rain, or the tides would turn and sink so low fishing became impossible at the end of the jetty. The inclement weather matched many a mood that first fishing season. I too was at low tide.

Live bait was often a problem. At that time I did not realize the pin-fish was a great bait—that I held the answer to catching my dream of a Snook right there in my hand.

I was fortunate to have a great college-Eckerd College, right down the block.

As an alumni, I often attended guest lectures, especially anything involving fish or Marine Biology. Marine Biologists, studying the diets of the Snook; have sliced open their stomachs and analyzed the contents – low and behold –pin-fish are the food of choice found most often inside the Snook. Sometimes the answer is right in front of our eyes.

During the terrible Red Tide of 2005, shrimp were scarce, and I did not yet understand or trust in lures, nor had I been introduced to the cast net, a useful tool in the constant, unceasing battle of finding live bait to catch big fish.

Somehow I kept the dream alive, and the dream kept something inside me alive. It stoked the glowing coals of desire, and kept the fires, however low and banked, burning. Always, I kept an eye on the tides. I knew a change would come, and when it did, I would be ready. So I stayed home and studied. I leaned everything I could about Snook. Where to find them, how to catch them—their habits, their habitat and best baits to use. Wait and the tide will turn. During the lows, I took the time to study the phases of the moon and the turn of the tides, and discovered that fishing was better on certain days of the month, so I began to put what free time I did have to particularly good use.

Bypassing the average days, when everyone else was out fishing, I awaited patiently my chance to fish those days of the month when the moon and the tides were in conjunction with the minor and major Solurnars, a specific time each day and night, when the fish begin to bite as if on cue each day, then I struck with a vengeance, sneaking out early and late. And I caught fish. Lots of fish. Still no Snook, but Jacks and trout and even redfish, each in a different way, learning from each.

Everything by chance at first, but then I began to detect, through trial and error, and the certainty of experience, a subtle pattern emerging. I caught more big fish at certain times of the morning and evening, and if I waited for the tides to change, especially the transition tides, the expected occurred like clockwork, like big fish biting non-stop.

I kept a journal, a notation to myself, registering critical data, facts and details, which I scrutinized religiously.

I bought a calendar that showed the phases of the moon each month and paid particular attention to the waning and waxing moons. I marked the days and the weeks when the big fish were biting. Each month a predictable cycle repeated itself, and predictably certain fish would bite.

In this way I learned to wait out the bad days, the scarcity of bait, the unpredictability of the weather, and became content with my life at the time. I worked with my father on his physical therapy while I studied and researched everything I could about fishing.

In this way, the wait became its own reward: I found Peace. Peace at the center of the storm.

6 Eye Of The Storm

My thoughts drift back to the flats at Fort Desoto, 2004. A sudden loneliness encompasses me, as once again I see the austere play of light and shadow slanting through the Australian pines, tinged with the last rays of the setting sun, which dips out of sight below the horizon of the mangrove islands to the west.

Darkness rides in on the wings of an Osprey. It swoops down to hook a fish in its talons, then soars back up again to stand sentinel atop a tall pine, a speck of silver set against a gray, tarnished sky.

It has procured a trout from the edges, which line the deep pot-holes of the flats, not the white sandy bottom where I have been fishing, and I am forced to make adjustments.

I'm alone out here, in the afterglow of sunset casting out my line. I was fishing directly over the middle of the sand, but now I change my strategy. Any fish swimming across the white sandy bottom of the pot-hole, is perceptible to a bird of prey. Therefore, they inhabit the safer regions, outside the holes, hidden in the turtle grass where they would be less vulnerable. I have learned this lesson. I reel in and cast out again, this time hitting the outer edges—bull's eye!

The wind whispers across the flats, ruffling the water like the hands of a lover running over it. The water has turned a deep jade color, mingled with a fluid molten gold, touched with an under-layer of indigo, a shade shy of violet.

In the depths, flashes of silver flit through the turtle grass: Speckled Trout--my targeted species. The bobber, adjusted to reach the depths where the big gator trout school, drifts amicably on the tide, yet I get no bite.

Just as well, as my mind is on other things today…

The hurricane season is almost over, or so we thought. Several hurricanes have already brushed us by, including Charley, which was heading straight for us, then veered by one degree at the last moment and wiped out a good portion of Florida. Another two hurricanes have left us, here on St. Pete Beach, without electricity, and in the dark for days. With the sudden advent of one storm after another, the state of Florida is in a state of shock. We watch every storm approaching as if it is heading straight for us with a vengeance.

A monstrous new hurricane has made landfall on the east coast and is heading due west, in our direction. Although it could not miss us because it's so gigantic it covers the entire state of Florida on the map on the weather channel.

For the moment, however, out here, all is bewitchingly still, and eerily calm. The mangrove islands, where the secret Snook are stacked up till spring and the big Reds school along the oyster beds, is shrouded in mist. A strong storm on a rising or falling barometer, is often an excellent indication of fish bite, so I have come out here to fish—in the eye of the hurricane.

The constant storms of 2004 have left me battered, weary, bone-tired. I have been let go from my job at the University, so I am jobless, adrift; I am in the midst of a divorce, so I am without a family as well; my father lies on his death bed, gray as a ghost, the light fading from his eyes. The storms of life have come.

The only sound on the flats is the gurgling of my aerator hung on the bait bucket, and the lonely scree of the gulls blown inland, off course.

Due to the storm, the shrimpers' boats have remained inshore today, so I have cast out my net and caught a few sand perch near the shore.

A Great Blue Heron strides along the sands of a secluded cove, which sweeps in a semicircle, north toward the sea. In the distance, gray breakers roll in on a storm surge, crashing on the far shore. The fallen trunks of storm-tossed trees, lay bleached by the sun, worn smooth by the wind, their stark denuded branches reaching out like skeletal fingers, spindrift from the many storms.

An ill and unfavorable wind is driven from the east today, probably from the northeast quadrant of the hurricane, not a particularly auspicious wind for fishing.

The sun sinks below the tree-line and the darkness is settling all around. A few stars sprinkle the sky; a new moon pins up the shadows of night. I cast out one last time and my bobber lands on the darkening water. It drifts on a widening circle of ripples, as I borne far from my troubles at home, drift with it.

The storm is coming. I can feel the wind picking up, freshening the breeze in my face, the taste of salt on my tongue.

I've caught nothing this evening, at least not by way of a corporeal fish—a Trout or Redfish or even Snook. This day I have caught a far other fish. In the chiaroscuro of twilight, between the darkness and the light, there spreads a panorama of sea and sky, which at certain indefinable moments, parts to unveil the infinite in a reflection of the clouds on water, and which for a brief and tantalizing moment, has caught me unawares.

I turn in a full circle and behold the world spinning on its axis and I along with it.

And for a moment in time, I feel myself a part of something greater. Though landed, grounded to this earth, I too am a speck of spindrift blown before the storm, drifting on a larger sea and suddenly---I am trolling amid the stars.

Cast out, cast out, into that vaster, wider sea. Open your bail and let go.

With wars and rumors of wars, and pestilence and pandemics, not to mention terrorists armed with God knows what, as we are blown ever closer towards Armageddon, there is still a peace at the center of the storm, tranquility in the eye of the hurricane. I am a fisherman who has walked upon those troubled waters, I should know.

7 Flat-line: Lesson Of The Flats

The reason I moved out onto the flats was for a change of luck. Sometimes all you need is a move for it to improve. When the tide was low, I would wade out up to my ankles in the middle of the grass flats at Fort Desoto to try and catch a fish, any fish. Perhaps it was not so much a fish for which I was searching as something I was in danger of losing—my dreams.

As always, for all my troubles, the pin-fish were waiting. Waiting to ensnare me and drag me down or steal my bait. Many people and situations are eerily similar, just waiting to drag you down to the rocks. People who make promises, they never fulfill, full of hot-air, big talk. In the end, they steal your time and energy and leave you with nothing to show for it. On the rocks again.

And that led me to my next lesson: futility. I had to go to the flats to find it: flatline, the death of dreams. I had been preparing myself, as I studied different tackle, various baits and tactics. I learned to fish through all sorts of tidal and lunar weather conditions, when the big fish did strike again, I would be prepared.

But I was not prepared for futility. The death of dreams: "Unless a seed fall into the earth and die it will not grow…"

I knew when to catch a big fish, now I had to learn how. Only then would I be ready. If you try to catch them before your time, you may get lucky and catch one, but chances are you will lose them more often than not.

The one aspect, which still eluded me was a thorough understanding of knots. In the beginning I had no idea they meant so much. This ignorance would lead to my undoing and to my salvation.

After months of fishing the flats and catching nothing but pin-fish, my patience was wearing thin. For a time I called it quits. Hung up my rod and reel. The dream died of natural causes. It seemed pointless to go on. Futile.

In addition, my father's condition worsened. While trying to walk, he lost his balance and fell on his face. Fortunately his knees broke his fall, and the only injury was a bruised knee, but for a while, he decided not to get up and try again; he crawled back to his bed, and lay there quietly, his big dream of walking again--lost. When he did get up he sat in his wheelchair, staring out the window waiting to die.

He too had almost given up. With a broken knee it seemed pointless to go on.

His mind wandered amid strange dreams. He wandered in an empty church, whose doors were locked, walking through the rooms, calling out his dead mother's name, "Genevieve, Genevieve, Genevieve…"

I tried to help, but only in the little things. Like the little fish I had not yet given him my all. I was fearful and plagued by fear and doubt; consequently, I backed off and kept my distance. He quickly began to fade. His skin and his eyes turned ashen gray. His teeth and his hair fell out as the Radiation from the chemo razed his body and spirit. He gazed out at the world with the thousand yard stare of the doomed. And still I did nothing.

This much I have learned from fishing: Unless and until you are engaged in a big way—a burning passion, your dreams will die; you will be going through the motions, whatever you are doing, going to work, making love, fishing untouched by the beauty and wonder of life all around you.

Yet they must die for you to grow.

Life is not in the little things as some have said, but in the big dreams and burning desires of those people who dare to dream big, which, when properly directed, gives meaning to our lives.

To achieve the big dream, you must be willing to overcome futility. The feeling that it is all for nothing. The one I experience out there on the flats, day after day, catching nothing but pin-fish. You must overcome that empty feeling, and still give it your all in spite of everything.

It will take all your courage, all your compassion, your intellect--all your heart. Whatever your dream, a happy marriage, a promotion at work, fame, fortune, a big fish, or saving your father, success will not come by idly sitting on the rocks and waiting for your luck to change.

You must do your part, and grow--remain actively engaged to fulfill your dream, or you will be left with nothing but a sense of futility. Hopeless, useless- in vain.

And a dream is never in vain.

Ignore the small fish; if that is all you seem to be catching, pull your line out of the water wherever you are fishing and get up and try somewhere else. If all you get are more nibbles, try again, and again, until you find somewhere the big fish are biting. The small ones are a mere distraction, an utter waste of time-leading to futility.

Some people are content with catching anything, with any kind of luck, but the ones who dream big are not willing to settle for anything less. It is anathema.

With my own eyes, I have seen fishermen sit on the rocks all day, or wade lost in the flats and catch nothing but small fish, trying to pretend for whatever reasons that they are content to just sit there--that the big one might come along someday, while all around them, other fisherman are catching big fish; I was one of those fisherman of futility; I had to grow or I would have died out there on the flats clinging to false hope.

But I did not know how to grow. I just knew I stood in the middle of nowhere with nothing.

NOVEMBER 1, 2003 : The weather is unseasonably warm. I have fished the flats for months, but the cold fronts have not yet begun to move in, so I've quit. I tell myself I never want to go fishing again. Slowly, the dream has died, and I sit by myself, stagnant and unresponsive, looking out the window at the other fisherman.

Yet, as I drive by the water that surrounds me on both sides, to the east Boca Ciega Bay, the Gulf to the west, I unconsciously find myself studying the tides, checking the seabirds on the horizon.

I can't help myself. Even if it is pointless, I want to go fishing. I'm knee-deep in it now, and when I do—a miracle occurs.

8 Knee Deep In It: Lesson Of The Ladyfish

It was in the air, in the cry of the seabirds. As I sat in my comfortable lazy-boy, watching TV, I heard a distant echo of sea-music from afar, the sounds of gulls, thousands of them. I tried to ignore the sound, to tell myself it meant nothing to me anymore, but I could not.

If you keep your ear attuned to the sound, sometimes the dream refuses to die.

I took my rod and reel down from the wall and ran, not walked to the eastern seawall. Sea-birds crowded the sky, diving, swooping, plunging into the water and resurfacing, beaks laden with quivering silver. Instinctively, I gazed beneath the surface. I could not believe my eyes. Thousands upon thousands of glass minnows, small baitfish, congregated near the rocks. Along the outer, impenetrable darker edges, where the water line divides the deeper blue from the shallower, transparent green, schools of sizeable fish left wide swaths of white-water in their wake.

The entire bay rippled with marine life, roiling with schools of ravenous fish everywhere.

I stood on the sea-wall, baited a hook and cast out into the blue. Instantly, at least a dozen fish, of varying species, Ladyfish, Bluefish and Spanish Mackerel, assaulted my hook, and seized my shrimp, each fighting each other to be the first.

The reel wailed as my line, tethered to a slashing, flashing bolt of silver-blue, ran out, through the crystal clear, aquamarine waters, un-spooling yards of line in seconds.

I yanked back—hard and set the hook. It went airborne, a Ladyfish in a fury of froth, leapt from the water, again and again and again.

I released it, baited up and cast out—as soon as the hook hit the water-another strike—this time a large Bluefish tore through the water, lashing out ferociously.

My children wanted in on the fun, but there were three of us, and I had only thought to bring two poles rigged and ready for action. I handed one to my son, Sky, rigged with a red and white bomber. He cast out—two fish hit simultaneously, hooked in the front and back tremble hooks at once. He reeled them in happily, pulled them off, released them and cast out again. Wham! Another hit, then another and another. Incredibly, this time he had three fish on, one on each treble hook. The pole was ripped from his hands and I watched as my expensive rig swam away before my eyes, carried by three large fish.

I leapt down from the wall and retrieved it. I cut off the bomber, and replaced it with a hook. I did not have time to de-hook three fish every time he cast out. One hook at a time would have to do. Saltwater is deadly on a reel, but I'd wash the salt out of it later. I was busy.

When I climbed back up, my daughter Phoebe sang out, "my turn."

Diplomatically, I suggested Sky share his pole with his sister, but he would have none of it.

"Why don't you give her yours," he laughed as my face fell.

The tug of a large Ladyfish almost yanked Sky off the wall. It zig-zagged out of the water and swept him southward down the length of the seawall, as he hung on for dear life.

"Fish on!" He shouted. "Ladyfish."

He leapt off the wall, and hit the beach in full stride, where he fished it from the shore-line. The dolphins were channeling schools of fish in a feeding frenzy.

Instead of the usual diving and slipping gently through the waves parallel to shore, these dolphin were aggressively feeding. Straight at my son they shot, dorsal fins cutting a swath through the water. Stopping a few feet shy of him, the dolphins channeled the school of fish toward the shore, then, when they had them cornered, threw the fish up into the air, playing with them before they swallowed them in one mouthful. My son jumped back just in time, soaked from head to foot.

A cycle of chaos ensued: gulls swooping and dashing above the bay, churning glass-minnows into a roiling dark cloud in the water; swarms of Ladyfish, gorging themselves on glass minnows; dolphin relentlessly running down everything in their path, leaving spumes of water in their wake. And amidst it all, a little boy chased them down, tossing out his line again and again and again, into the boiling, churning mass. Every time he cast out, he caught a Ladyfish.

Phoebe gazed at me impatiently.

"What?" I asked although I knew.

"You know what!" He blue eyes blazed.

I admit I was torn. The father and the fisherman struggled within me. The father won out. I handed her my rod, the lucky one that had caught the Snook, and she cast out.

As soon as her hook hit the water, the rod bent double. Calmly, unnaturally poised for a five year old, she reeled it in. She's a natural. A large Ladyfish. Beaming proudly, she sassily proclaimed that hers was bigger than her brothers.

"But I caught more," he shot back.

Not to be outdone, Sky baited up and cast out again—this time to my utter amazement he hooked up with a giant Snook, at least 44 inches, maybe 20 pounds.

As it leapt from the water it threw the hook. It zinged back empty. It caught in his shirt, and I had to cut it out of his sleeve with my Swiss Army knife.

"Give me another shrimp," he shouted. A fire I had never seen before lit the eyes of my nine year old. His hair was plastered to his face with sweat, his clothes bloodstained and now torn, his mouth set and determined. He had the fever now, the big dream was upon him.

The Snook is a magical and mysterious fish. Once hooked, you can never get him out of your mind. It stays there, swimming in the subterranean outgoing currents of the unconscious, then with a flick of its tail, dives back out of sight so deep it comes up only in our dreams, only to resurface again on the incoming tide of longing and desire.

But the Lady-fish, ah, the Ladyfish. Although some call it a trash-fish, the Lady-fish to me, is all desire. For it was she who brought back my dream, alive and swimming before my eyes. It was she who restored the miracle—the fun in fishing, the sheer delight of a leaping, jumping fish. I do not believe the name is an accident, for I have known women-the Lady-fish of the species, who have performed the same miracle on my spirit-who granted me the vision on my quest of errant knighthood to find the holy grail of fish-the Snook. It was the Lady-fish who gave me back my sight. Bless her.

As the frenzy continued, the bait bucket emptied fast. Three dozen shrimp gone in a matter of minutes. Gulped down, and swallowed whole. Fortunately, Phoebe, little pack-rat that she is, had thought to bring her net. She jumped down from the sea-wall and waded out, knee-deep into a swirling mass of glass-minnows. She scooped them up in her net and passed them up to us, proud to be of service to her older brother and her father.

Sky and I baited up and cast out—instantly, as if on cue, both of us hooked up at once, reeling in two Ladyfish together. We sang out happily-"Fish on."

We smiled and hi-fived each other as cars screeched to a halt, tourists got out and snapped photos or shot video, boats, large and small, paused, engines idling, as an eager audience watched enthralled.

Watching amid the multitude, was a woman, Hazel, who has lived on Pass-A-Grille since the 1950's. As I walked to get my morning paper the next morning, she informed me she had never seen anything like it. She also told me that as a little girl, in the 50's she had caught her first Snook off that very same wall, in the same spot, with a long-dead, legendary fisherman from Pass-A-Grille. He had known every place to catch the big ones, she mysteriously added. I wondered at the time if she meant that perhaps the big dream, the one that had eluded me for so long, had been right there under my nose.

The feeding frenzy occurred three days from the last quarter moon in April. It turned on at precisely 6:01 p.m. and lasted until a quarter till eight. In the interim my son, my daughter and I caught and released an average of one Ladyfish per minute. I made a note of time and place, but the miracle did not reoccur the following year nor do I think it will come again.

It's OK. I no longer require signs and wonders to keep me going. I have learned to walk by faith, trusting the everyday miracles right before my eyes. The so-called trash-fish, the humble Lady-fish, the Spanish Mackerel, the Blue-fish, which run in schools of thousands, are always there, like the sun rising in the east, as an affirmation, that even in the darkest times, grace and mercy abound. We're knee-deep in it.

During the chaos and confusion of that day, I tied and re-tied a never-ending series of knots, for every other fish we hooked weakened our already frayed line to the breaking point, or just snapped it in a dazzling display of aerial acrobatics.

In the heat of the moment, when the bite is on, you are flying blind. The sweat pours down your face, your fingers slick with blood and slime, your hands shaking with the adrenalin rush. Errant hooks snagged my fingers and I mistakenly touched a Skip Jack.

Its poison paralyzed my finger, and made it virtually impossible to thread a knot. I had to work my knots with stiff, tortured fingers, then pull it tight with my teeth, the pain shooting through my hand like liquid fire. Sometimes we are tested to see if we are worthy of the dream.

There we stood. Our bloody, sweat-soaked clothing pierced by the free-flying barbs of our hooks, as one after another, fish lunged up out of the water and broke loose in mid-air, or landed on the wall, thrashed about, slinging the prickly hooks, whip-like through the air, nabbing everything in their trajectory. Once embedded, itinerant hooks stick, so the only way to get them out is to cut them out, and by the end of the night, our clothes were in shreds. My right hand, bloodied by the bite of the sharp steel hooks and poisoned by the Skip Jack, curled up like an arthritic claw, yet still we fished on.

Bored with catching bait, Phoebe taunted us, throwing the glass-minnows, for which our outstretched hands reached in vain, back into the sea by the handful. Funny girl.

So we wandered down to the shore and waded out, knee-deep in schools of whirling, swirling fish. I opened my tackle box and threw everything we had at them: every lure and leader, every jig and top-water, every hook, line and sinker. The fish cleaned me out, snapping line and breaking off lures, shredding knots and fraying leaders, bending hooks and springing snaps, till there was nothing left to throw. My tackle box was empty. No, I had one large silver hook left. I tied it directly to my braided line and cast out, thinking no fish would ever bite an empty hook, but it was worth a try because I did not, I could not stop. As I trolled the hook in slowly—I caught a big Bluefish, its throat packed full of glass-minnows.

Life-like it or not, we're knee-deep in it, too often unprepared for the challenges we face on the way to our big dreams: a career setback, divorce or the death of a loved one. Loss. Trouble abounds. Sometimes you have to fish on through the blood, the sweat and the tears, with one hand if need be, on an empty hook. Sometimes, like the mustard seed, it's enough.

I had grown. I was ready.

9 The Snook Whisperer

He was an old salt, a ragged sort of fishing bum, someone you would not look at twice in public, yet there was an air about him, a quiet confidence to his bearing, which belied his shoddy appearance.

Butter-flying a fresh mullet (slicing open its stomach to cause it to sink), he whirs it above his head, as if he were slinging a shot put, and casts it out on his old, shitty rod and reel. I notice he gets his bait further out into the channel than anyone else fishing that day. He then wipes the blade of his bloody filleting knife on his old ragged, cut-offs, and sticks it in his back pocket.

His filthy denim shirt, open to the waist, is faded to a robin's egg blue; his shorts, stained with blood, hang off his lean, spare frame, except for a small gut, at odds with the rest of him.

His brown arms, deeply veined and stained the color of tobacco, stick out from under a grimy black T-shirt with the faded logo of a heavy metal band; his face, deeply tanned and lined, is gaunt and salt-silvered like his wisp of a beard, but his eyes are as bright blue as the blue ocean itself, with the rough edge of an undertow, darkening his glance like a storm at sea. He has an easy smile. And a cast net full of live bait-pin-fish to be exact.

It is said by the sages of old that, if you pursue your path long enough, with passion and with unswerving devotion, that when you are ready, a guide will miraculously appear, though not always as expected.

This was no well appointed fisherman stepping forth from the pages of a slick fishing magazine with all the fashionably correct gear and suitable clothing – he didn't even have a tackle box --this was a master fisherman with blood on his hands and fish scales on his cut-offs, a razor-sharp knife in his back pocket, to filet the fish he caught on the spot for dinner, and a strange, knowing smile, which seemed to suggest he was not what at first he appeared to be.

Of course, I completely ignored him.

Then he does something strange. He puts on a mask and flippers and dives off the end of the jetty. He swims out beyond the buoys and disappears into the deep, between the knife edge line of the shallower green and the darker blue water. He resurfaces with a huge tangled knot of fishing line. In it were hundreds of snagged lures, hooks, sinkers, jigs, everything he needed. He resurfaces with one in his hand—a nice Bomber. This man does not require an expensive tackle box full of the latest lures; he takes what the sea provides. It was to become my mantra. Today you can set me down anywhere with just one rig and two empty hooks, a large one and a small one. I will take what the sea provides, and catch my own bait and then catch a large fish. Anywhere, anytime.

When the Old Fisherman gets back to the jetty I'm curious, so I ask him how he knew he would find all that out there.

"I watched the other fisherman losing their rigs, all in the same place," he grins. "So I knew where to look."

The sun sets in a curtain of firelight, and his silhouette is framed against a red sky. I notice he has been watching me as well. At first, I feel revulsion. What does the old bum want? Probably wants to bum a smoke or "borrow" some bait or leader material.

How many times have I heard that? In Florida, many fishermen fish not for fun and sport, but to feed themselves. They never seem to bring their own stuff.

This man, however, has not asked me for a thing.

Here on the jetty, however, because it is Pass-a-Grille, once a community of poor fishermen who made their living from the sea, now an ulta- rich community of multi-million dollar homes, we honor fishermen of all kinds.

The well-heeled fishermen on the jetty sport all the latest gear and up-to date equipment: reels with names like Quantum, Shiamono or Fin Nor. Their open tackle boxes are bursting with bright shiny lures and every other expensive artificial. It takes me a while to realize they are not catching anything. Very few are using fresh bait or a cast-net like the old salt. They, like their lures are artificial.

And although I too am fishing an old, moth-eaten rod and cranky Penn reel that needs oiling, I am catching a few fish, and every once in a while the occasional medium sized Whiting. I notice he's watching me.

He walks up, looks down at me and shakes his head.

"You're not using the right hook, or line, or bait" he scoffs. "And your knot is not tied right, but the Snook are not going to bite anyway."

He talked as if he knew exactly what kind of fish I was fishing for. "This time of year you have to cast parallel to the shore to land Centropomus Undecimalis."

He was on a first name basis with the Snook!

At the time I had no earthly idea what he was talking about. I knew neither the nicknames nor the lore of Snook. I just wished he would go away.

"Don't worry," he assured me. "They're out there. You got to learn to let go. Open your bail and let it drift in the water. Free-line. "

"I've always heard it's best to keep a tight line?" I said. Ignoring him, I dug a small half-dead shrimp out of my bucket and hooked it through the stomach as I turned my back on him and prepared to cast out.

"Wait!" He looked as if he wanted to tear the fishing rod right of my hands.

"What!" Now I was really getting angry. What the hell does this old raggedy-ass bum want anyway? As if in answer to my question, he climbed down on the rocks with me and took the dead shrimp off my large silver hook.

"Don't belly hook your shrimp. They won't swim naturally, and the Snook won't bite, unless you get lucky. And most people aren't too lucky when it comes to Snook. You may get lucky once, but not twice."

"Oh." I said, my interest suddenly piqued. I had gotten lucky once, but not again, as he prophesied. This man was turning out to be more interesting than I thought. If he knew something about Snook, I was willing to drop my pride and listen. He looked and acted like he knew what he was talking about.

"Hook it just under the horn, or in the tail and let it go, but watch the black spot, those're its vitals."

"Try this. "He fished (no pun intended) into his pocket and took out a curved black hook, called a circle hook. It had a wicked edge. When I held it in my hand it was as light as a feather.

"Number 1, light wire. Hook'a shrimp to this, it presents naturally, fluttering in the current like a real shrimp. Snook's a predator.

He needs to chase something moving like it would in the water. A heavy hook makes your bait move awkwardly, sinks it right down to the bottom of the water column. Snook wants to see it swim."

Now he had me. As far as I was concerned, he was speaking in tongues, but it was becoming increasingly obvious he knew his subject: Snook.

Snicker Snack – a blade whirred. He whipped out a switchblade, cut my line at the leader.

Before I could protest he continued. "And don't use mono-filli-ment, it reflects the sunlight. Snook have good eyesight. "There's a new line on the market. Tinted fluorocarbon, can't see it – not even the sparkles, not even on a moonlit night. Get it. Use it."

Again, I had no clue. How had these fine points escaped me? I thought I was prepared. Ha!

The Old Salt dug into his shirt pocket and took out a coiled fluorocarbon leader; in a flash he looped both line and the leader together, expertly slipped them around each other, secured both tag ends into one seamless line to line knot, then slipped them down against the hook eye like a noose.

"How did you –" I would kneel at his feet and kiss the ground he walked on if he could teach me how to tie a knot like that.

With the impending darkness, I could not adequately see how he had accomplished this maneuver, as his old, gnarled fingers moved like quicksilver in the twilight.

"You want as little hardware as possible."

"Hardware. What was he talking about? The only hardware I knew lay on the shelves at Home Depo.

The old salt turned the hook sideways and slid it through the shrimp's horn near its head. Instead of lying there like it always did for me, it started jumping and snapping in mid-air, quite unlike the half-dead shrimp I had been presenting. No! this was a different bait altogether. It moved on the end of the hook. I wondered what it would look like underwater to a fish.

I was quite impressed; my first impressions of the man were changing by the minute. Was he actually going to help me catch a Snook? Oh, God. Please!

But the Old Salt was not yet done. He removed a paperclip from his shirt-pocket, adorned with colorful beads, something like a homemade, be-jeweled lure.

"This will help Mr. Snook find his way to you through dark, murky water."

He ripped my bobber off and slipped a tiny split-shot onto the line, then bit down on it in place with his teeth. So much for lead poisoning.

"Use the bobber for pinfish. For Snook, free-line. Not that Mr. Snook don't like structure, he does, but the big ones are out there in the surf. They're on the move this time of year, back to the flats."

"The flats!" I said astounded. I had quit fishing the flats only weeks before. I had given up in frustration, cursing my luck. Now I learn that's where the Snook are going! This was a revelation to me.

"Timing is everything," he confided with a wry half smile, as if to say, "that's right, you dumb shit," but he was far too courteous. "With your permission," he added graciously.

I nodded my assent. He took my rod and reel and cast out with a quick snap of the wrist; it sprung to life in his hand. The hook made hardly a ripple as it dropped into the sea parallel to the shore. With a quick, deft move, he reeled in a little.

He handed the rod back to me and I opened my bail and let it drift awhile like he said. Learning to let go.

We begin to talk.

"I was watching you," he said. You don't know what the hell you're doing, but you have the one thing every good fisherman has to have," he added sincerely with a touch to his heart.

"Patience?" I dutifully replied, suppressing the urge to scream.

"No -- passion." He stated matter of factly. "Your heart's in it. I heard you cursing every time you lost a fish. Reminds me of myself when I was a young dock rat."

"Oh." I said humbly - touched.

"All these other young fellas, they stand there and cast in, lose some, catch some, maybe catch nothing at all, makes no difference to them, cause they don't really care. All business, but to you fishing seems like life and death."

Little did he know how close to the bone his words had sliced.

"Just remember if you fish by luck, your luck can change from good to bad. Better to be prepared."

Yes. I was learning that. I was glad it had grown dark, because, his words had brought a tear to my eyes. He was right. Fishing had become a passion, mixed up somehow with my father and his impending death, my youth, all my hopes, my dreams, my aspirations. In fact these days, I would almost rather fish than eat or sleep.

Yet here was a man who was showing me how to have the faith to cast out and let go. I knew it now. That was what I'd been missing.

"Where's your rig," I asked him.

"When I fish I prefer to fish with my fingers," he stated matter of factly.

The words rang like an explosion in my head. "What?"

"All the old-timers do it. Gives you a feel for it. Out from your heart, through your fingertips, into the sea. One touch, and I know what I've got on the other end."

"Who are you?" I asked intrigued.

"Name's Tom. Commercial fisherman, out of the Keys." His warm brown voice, a whiskey-soaked rasp, was soothing in the twilight. The things he said made sense.

"Fishermen are full of surprises," he laughed and his blue eyes sparkled like the sun on the sea.

A sudden hard jerk on the line informed me it was time to refocus my attention.

While we had been talking, my line had snapped taught. After a hard fight, I reeled in a 24 inch silver fish with black stripes. It put up a good stiff fight. A marked improvement over pin-fish.

"Look, I caught a Sheepshead," I said, trying to sound well-versed, hoping to impress the Old Salt. See! I know my fish.

"Nah, that's a drum." He pointed to the stripes. "Sheepshead have seven stripes, Drum, five. Been in jail longer."

Right. It's a drum, five, a Sheepshead -seven. Damn! He was good.

"How do you know so much about fish?"

"All I do," he answered. "Come down to Key West and I'll take you fishing sometime. Or maybe blue water, fishing for Blue Marlin off of Cuba, now there's a fish! Takes two or three hours to catch, leaps maybe 40, 50 times. Break your back trying to pull it up. Spent a lot of nights sleeping on my stomach."

"Sounds like fun," I said, although at the time I was too consumed with Snook. Later, however, I resolved to take him up on his offer.
"Mostly I fish for Red Snapper, out of the Vaca Cut in Marathon. Caught six-hundred pounds with my fingers. He held up two fingers on his huge scarred hand. Hundreds of fish at a time. One after another, all night, and I still love it. Bought me a nice boat, which I live on most of the time. Don't know a good diesel mechanic do you?"

"No." I said. Sorry. At the moment a boat is something I can only dream of, but I seem to dream of it a lot these days."

"Well, dreams have a way of coming true if you follow them long enough," he answered with a kind smile that made me want to beg his forgiveness for misjudging him earlier.

"What's the name of your boat?" I asked.

"My boat has no name," he added mysteriously.

A sudden strike on the line brought me back again. A small Snook leaped out of the waves. It's small-- but it's a Snook, and my heart leaps with it.

"I caught one." I shouted. "A Snook!" I cried. I wanted to kiss the man.

"Gotta land it first." He warned. When I turn back to him, the old salt is walking away down the sandy path.

I could see the vague outline of his head and shoulders, becoming as indistinct as the daylight among the sea oats on the dunes. As he melted back into the shadows, I wondered if he were real after all or just a figment of my imagination. Something I have called forth, conjured into being to help me in my time of need.

I turn back to the fish, and my line goes slack. I have lost another Snook.

"I lost him," I shout into the shadows.

"Get some good braid." Comes the echoing reply.

I turn back to the sea, now as dark as night. I can see the reflection of the stars in the tidal pools around the rocks, and suddenly I feel alive. My pole, like an extension of my arm, is by my side, the broken line fluttering lightly in the breeze, but my spirit is soaring up there with the stars.

What is braid? I wonder. And he mentioned something about Snook on the flats. And the way he tied that knot onto the hook, sliding it down to the eye, so that the harder the fish fought, the tighter it cinched the knot. Although I lost the Snook, it wasn't the knot that broke this time; it was his and it held – the Snook had thrown the hook. I make a mental note. I need stronger line, something the old salt called braid. I will get some.

There's three basics to consider, the Old Salt mused, when stalking Snook: 1). BAIT: match the hatch, whatever's in the water: greenbacks, spanish sardines, pin-fish, Ladyfish, or shrimp; 2). TEMPERATURE: when the water hits the magic 70 degrees, the Snook bite explodes; when it gets colder, Snook migrate up rivers and under mangroves.3).STRUCTURAL PATTERNS: jetties, docks, piers and bridges, and along the beaches-sandbars."

Somewhere in my mind a light switches on. Cause and effect. Suddenly I'm catching bigger fish. I hooked another Snook, and although I lost it, I did land a medium sized Black Drum.

With a few words, a few simple actions, which otherwise might have taken me a life-time to learn, the Old Salt has taken me on my first steps toward becoming more than a recreational fisherman, he has taken me under his wing and indoctrinated me into an ageless club. He has made me a fisherman.

One day perhaps I will take him up on his offer in the Keys, but today is it sufficient to know that I can catch fish. For now I will move back to the flats to follow my elusive dream. I thank him silently as the darkness merges from the fading violet of twilight into the black velvet stillness of night, and all is lost in its shadows.

"Wait!" I cry out.

He turns and looks back, waiting, his profile indistinct in the twilight.

"I want to fight, catch and land a big fish!"

He walks back towards me like a phantom out of the night. "First you must learn to whisper their secret name."

He leans in and whispered something in my ear. "You're not fighting a fish, you're fighting yourself. Fish on!.

10 Black Spot: Lesson Of The Redfish

JANUARY 1, 2004: LATE AFTERNOON, the flats are cold, empty and somber today: Autumn has turned a page to winter, and brought with it, an overcast sky reflected in the dull water of muted silver. I'm alone on the flats, standing in dark, knee-deep water as I cast out my line. It gets lost in the silver reflection of the silver clouds.

Fort Desoto, in St. Petersburg, Florida, designated as the number one family beach in the United States, is a tangle of winding waterways, grass flats, oyster bars and mangroves, a natural habitat for every species of inshore game fish, so this is where I have moved to perfect the art and craft of fishing.

Here on the northern shore, the waves break on miles of deserted white beaches. Beyond the mangrove islands, the wind blows plumes of sand off the crests of the dunes, which the hurricanes have piled high with sand.

This afternoon I have wandered into an enchanted place. From the beach, I turned inland, following a winding river into a little cove, an estuary, which is a breeding ground for the Speckled Sea Trout, the Redfish and of course, like the Old Salt suggested – schools of returning Snook. I'm hoping he was right.

I wade through a pass flushed with cold, clear water, which flows past the mangroves to the sea, past a small Osprey's island to the west, past an oyster bar close to an inner bay of grass flats, hiding deep holes in the center. As I walk I cast out, covering a wide area. I retrieve my top-water slowly as the fish will be lethargic from the cold.

When I see a school of redfish, I always cast out ahead of them, then pull my bait back in almost in front of their noses. Never cast into the school itself, as you will spook it, and they will move on. Pick them off on the periphery.

In the branches of an Australian pine, an ever-present Osprey stands outlined against the sky. It flaps his wings, disengages from its nest and flies away over the flats into the lining of a silver cloud where it becomes invisible. A good omen, for birds of prey are the ultimate fishermen, and where they roost, there is sure to be fish.

As I stroll along, I look down through the water and notice a set of giant, three-toed footprints embedded in the muck, a sign of the presence of the great Blue Heron, another bird whose instincts tell it where to fish; I follow in its footsteps to the oyster bar and cast out in the deeper holes, alone and isolated out here with nothing but my thoughts.

The mullet begin to leap all over the flats; I can see their fins cutting the water.

My pole bends double – fish on. A speckled sea trout lunges up and rises out of the water, then under again, in a flash of silver, yanking the tip of my rod down as it runs out to sea across the flats. I try to reel it back in, but in my excitement I "horse it," fisherman lingo for overplaying a fish, and my line goes slack. Trout, because of the delicacy of their mouths, must be played subtly, even-handedly, reeling in slowly and surely.

A sudden loneliness encompasses me. The wind whispers across the flats. The air, stark and cold, raises the tiny hairs along my arm.

The sun has long since gone down behind the trees to the west, and I have been too preoccupied to notice I am standing knee-deep in the middle of the flats. I've waded out deep without knowing it.

In the pale winter light, reflecting off the water, a subtle shift of shadow has occurred, silvering everything. Only the trees on the island and the dunes beyond have darkened in a ring along the periphery of the estuary to the east.

Out here is a refuge from the daily regimen of pills and prescriptions, the doctor's waiting room, the nurse's blood tests, the hospital check-ups, the weekly chemotherapy-treatments, the endless Hospice volunteers, a never-ending entourage of sickness and contagion.

All winter the estuary is my sanctuary, while I attempt to fulfill the requirements of an Inshore Slam. My daughter keeps telling me it will happen.

"You can do it," she says, and I realize, to succeed, to really accomplish your goals and objectives in life, it is good to have a cheerleader. Someone on your side, someone who cares.

On reflection, I realize my ex-wife never went fishing with me. Not once! I was not asking much, just a little of her time and interest, but it was not to be. Yet I was expected to be a loving husband, an excellent provider, a kind and caring father, a great conversationalist, a good dancer, everything to make her dreams come true.

I attended her art openings, sat through escargot and vichyssoise, Crovassier and caviar, pretending to listen to the small talk among the art and crafts crowd, smiled sincerely and nodded my head in all the right places.

Don't get me wrong; I'm not a fisherman who lacks culture, nor am I against art, as long as it is worthy, but the over-hyped world of arts and crafts just doesn't do it for me. I have traveled to the great art museums of the world and seen with my own eyes, the genius of Van Gogh, in the forests of the Rijks Museum; beheld the dark monsters of Goya in the Prado in Madrid; contemplated DaVinci's masterpiece, the Mona Lisa, at the Louve; stared in wonder at Rothko's luminous shape-shifting geometric compositions at the Tate Gallery in London; yet to me, most wonderous of all, the primitive cave art at Altimira and Lescaux. The so-called primitives—hunters and fishermen like me.

But at least I tried. For her. She did not do the same for me. It was all one-sided.

I make a vow never to date anyone who doesn't like to fish, who refuses to participate in my dream. To accomplish the Inshore Slam, a fisherman must catch all three inshore species of fish: Trout, Redfish and Snook, in a single day. I caught both the trout and the Redfish, but still the elusive Snook evaded me, spoiling my dreams. In the end the flats became something of a true disappointment.

For the most part, they were just that—flat, monotonous, often tedious, but the occasional strike, plus the experience of hands-on learning kept me coming back. That and the lonely sensation of delight of being out there alone at sunset, stalking the fish of my dreams. Often the water was calm, glassy, mirror smooth.

And as I cast out, my bobber would drop with a tremor into the water, and drift on an ever-widening circle of ripples, until it darkened, a reflection of the sunset itself. Whoever invented time, must not have been a fisherman.

One night, the ever-present Osprey, which stood sentinel in the treetops, swooped, tipped its wing and slashed into the water right over a deep hole in the middle of the flats. It mounted up, a silver trout clutched in its talons. I can see it, standing tall and proud, outlined against the sky, picking apart the fish with its beak, as everything deepens into twilight on the idyllic island.

Out here I learn by watching and interpreting, not as before, from what I have read in a book, or from what I thought I knew, but from what I observe nature has to teach. Because he is a better fisherman than I, I fish where the Osprey fishes.

As a result I reel in a small speckled trout, about 19 inches long and toss it onto the shore. I do not have a stringer and a raccoon, ambling along the banks swipes it in his paw, and lopes back into the shadows of the mangroves.

But at least I have finally caught a trout. Now I need a Redfish, so I wade over to the oyster bar. I have begun to think like a fish. I have yet to catch a Redfish or a Snook, however, and it clouds my sense of accomplishment.

Rosette Spoonbills line the banks; their pink plumage backlit by the setting sun, all aglow like feathered silk. Anhingas, standing along the half-sunken driftwood branches of fallen trees, lift their wings to dry in the sun. Again and again, I cast out my line and watch it arc against a high, white cumulonimbus cloud, which billows out against the sky, before it falls out near the oyster bar.

I watch a school of mullet swimming by, hidden to the unseeing eyes of a man who has never looked below the facade of everyday appearances, and I suddenly know I will get a bite. How I know this, I cannot tell, but I do—the water just looks right –sure enough a big Redfish is on! I reel him in and look at him.

He's big with a black spot on his tail. I'm happy. This proves I'm getting better. In fact, now that I've caught a trout and a red-fish I'm two thirds to an Inshore Slam. I'm a good fisherman, and I'm getting better.

But a Snook is a different kind of fish altogether.

A fisherman learns to see beneath the surface of things, to spot fish where they swim, to gage which way the tide is flowing, incoming or outgoing, the fish around the oyster bars, the drop offs in the passes where Snook might lay in wait for a well-placed bait. Out here, I have learned to see things differently. Something about that black spot on the Red-fish's tail bothers me. To me it's a symbol writ large. The black spot is a blemish on my record—it serves to remind me that I have yet to catch a Snook. Only then will I be a champion!

With reverent eyes, I comprehend the Creator and his creation, and I see that it is a deep sea, with an even deeper drop-off, which is unfathomable. And I am fishing it.

Yes, I have seen with eyes that have looked upon death, and I have gazed beneath the surface into the depths where the big fish swim. It is lonely and dark, a place where no light shines, except the light of dead stars. Way down deep my foot has touched bottom, and I have come up again for air, and turned my face toward the sun, toward life, toward hope.

But in going so deep I have caught the bends and I have felt the dark side, which no one ever wants to talk about: depression and divorce—even suicide, it's all down there in the deep. I had to fight to follow the light back to the surface.

One thing leads to another, and by these signs we find our way. The Mullet precede the Redfish as sure as night follows day. Find an oyster bar. Use a light leader and a shrimp to catch red-fish. It's almost too easy.

These insights, which lie just beneath the surface, are available to everyone. But you must stop and listen to what's around you. You can't touch them, hold them, see or smell them, but they are there just the same, invisible to the naked eye, but to the eye of the fisherman, ever-present.

The black spot is death to my dreams. "To be good is not enough when you dream of being great."

Columbus must have been a fisherman, for almost alone among his peers, he was a man who understood that the earth was not flat. That the seas curved, and that some force—gravity held everything in its place. A bold adventurer, he was not afraid to set out into the unknown, when everyone else told him he would fall off the edge of the world. He must've sensed, from careful observation, a circular pattern to the tides and seasons, for his eyes saw beyond the horizon to a new world. And I have seen a new world as well, out here as well—as a fisherman. I have caught a redfish now.

I am lulled, however, by a false sense of accomplishment, for although I have caught two of the coveted species in a Slam, they are not my ultimate goal. They are mere stepping stones on the way to the bigger dream.

Fish strike, even some relatively big ones once in a while, to hold my interest, but nothing extraordinary, and that's the problem. It's nice out here on the flats, yet almost mediocre. One can easily grow stagnant. I wade into the heart of the mangroves in search of Snook and the fulfillment of my goal of an Inshore Slam, but once I've achieved that dream, what then?

While the flats may seem appealing at the moment, they are very dangerous because they seem so perfect. In truth, the flats are anathema to big dreams.

They are not full of holes for nothing. Deep black holes into which the errant wader may fall if he does not watch his step, sucked down into the mire, with grass and weeds entwined.

I have spent the better part of a year and a half out here, and have not yet advanced to the Grand Slam. Although I have caught a few big trout – gator trout as they are called, and it was a great thrill, something does not feel right. Out here I am merely a dreamer, not a doer. And therein lies another lesson.

Big dreams come to us for a reason with a purpose, not to get lost in the dream itself, however enticing, but to move towards that which we desire with all our heart. A dream is a beautiful thing, but if it never comes to fruition, it remains a dream, nothing more. No one is cured of Polio, Yellow Fever or Small Pox, no one takes to the skies on the wings of Kitty Hawk, or leaves his footprints upon the moon.

My dream is a Snook. Not a trout, not a Redfish. A Snook, and I will settle for nothing less.

Time spent in the flats will wrap you in its dream-like embrace, enfolding you in a world that is more fantasy than real.

I've fished the flats all winter and caught nothing more substantial than 19-22 inch trout and a 24 inch Redfish to feed the hunger-fever of my dream. But I have not seen one Snook. Not one all winter. Yet it's so beautiful and peaceful out here--and therein lies the danger, I have almost forgotten about my dream; lulled into a deep and dreamless slumber I almost want to forget. It's a bother and a nuisance to dream. Why not just go to sleep?

Wake up! Once you enter the land of the lotus eaters, you're finished. Comfort and security comes like a thief in the night to rob you of all that matters. Your dream floats away in the mist, as you wave it goodbye.

Out here in this dreamy interlude, I'm inclined to settle for less because it's so much easier to stop and enjoy what I have done. Sure I've learned to catch fish out here - no problem, so I'm seduced by the reliable comfort of the flats. The big dream is a challenge, so I begin to make excuses why I'll never catch a Snook in my life, because I have grown complacent.

Why not sit back and enjoy what I have achieved? One year ago this would have been unthinkable. Catching big trout and a big Red in the same day?

The fisherman who sat on the rocks all day to catch one small fish? I've come a long way. Only one problem—I've begun to feel stranded on the flats.

Most people live their lives stranded on the flats of lost dreams. They measure their lives by the clock, going to work, getting married, buying a car, paying the mortgage, until little by little, the big dream slips away, leaving a smaller yet more comforting one to take its place. I've got everything I want don't I? Yet something nags deep within. What about the Snook?

There's no longer any challenge, merely a monotonous, flat routine, a compulsory rut known as the rat-race, a celebration of the ordinary: to work and back again, buying and getting almost everything we want and learning to settle for it, until the inevitable heart attack or cancer or whatever is eating us from the inside out strikes us down.

It's no accident heart disease is the number one killer in the United States, for it is a disease of the heart we have.

We have been trading away our lives on the flats of little dreams, settling for something almost comparable yet not quite equal to that original cry of love, which was wrung from our hearts in the very beginning. We look up one day and the big dream seems suddenly smaller. Where has it gone? The flats.

A big black hole lies at the center of our lives. We run to and fro, compulsive consumers, buying things at shopping malls, attending barbeques, partying, eating and drinking, as if through the acquisition of consumer goods, we might deaden the pain in our heart, which we so desperately try to hide. For we have lost our dreams, the big ones, the only ones that matter.

When we sacrifice the big dream within us, something inside us dies.

Each new possession is merely a replacement for the heart that used to beat with a passion for a big dream, and so we are seduced into settling for less, and little by little, the big golden fish with the long black stripe swims away before our eyes, and the little silver trout, the red-fish with the black spot, takes their place.

Those who willingly give in will never get the chance to see the world turn on its axis, and they'll never catch the big fish out on the edge of the world.

They stay on the flats and pretend to be content with the average, the common, the ordinary. Not for nothing, that the moment of your death, are you pronounced flat-line.

I dated a woman for awhile who shall remain nameless, in anonymity where she belongs. She did not like to fish. Far too sophisticated for that. When I asked her to come fishing with me, she looked at me as if I had to be kidding.

"Fishing? I want to go dancing," she said. "Come dancing with me."

She wanted more than I was willing to give without getting something in return. I just wanted to go fishing with someone. She wanted security, marriage, the ring on her finger, before she could begin to live and commit her heart to me. I loved her, but I had to move on. Her dreams were too small. As flat as her view of the earth. I wanted to set sail beyond the horizon, she was afraid we would fall off it.

Make no misunderstanding, marriage and children are a worthy goal, a big dream in and of itself. One of the biggest in fact. But only if you intend to give it your all.

To raise your children yourself, not drop them off at the nearest Day Care when they are six months old. To rock them to sleep at night, tell them bedtime stories, give them the gift of yourselves. For it is you they want, that thing inside, which makes you unique to their life—only you can give them that.

If you have married a trophy wife and moved into a trophy house, with an expensive mortgage to go with it, and have produced 2.5 trophy children, which you rarely, if ever see, except to drive to soccer practice, baseball practice, gym, music, or some other form of practice, because you are too busy, then go ahead -buy another couch, another big-screen TV or a new car and bury yourself deeper in the flat-line. You may win two out of three in the Inshore Slam, but you have lost the big one of your dreams.

Wives, if you want a dream marriage, give your husband everything. Hold nothing back; husbands, if you want a dream wife, give her everything and more. Love her with all your heart. If he loves golf, learn to play and go with him. If it's fishing he loves, learn how to throw a cast net and help him catch his bait--you will catch him forever.

Regarding children, I have two, so I can speak to that. A soft-spoken, down to earth boy named Sky and a precocious girl of five, Phoebe.

I love them with all my heart, and I give them my heart. They were not sent to school or Day Care until they were four years old, having spent their formative years with me, instead of some cranky, burned-out, overworked and underpaid, teacher's aid. I have a Masters Degree in English, and I taught my son the alphabet in the sand before he could walk as the waves washed it away.

He could read and write by the time he was three. He kept a journal, went to libraries; I watched over him and made sure he read great literature. While other kids were reading Itsy Bitsy Spider, or Aurthur the Ardvark, we were reading the classics, including Ernest

Hemingway's, <u>The Old Man and the Sea,</u> and Homer's <u>The Illiad</u>. That is part of who I am, what I have to give. And, always I have taken him fishing with me at all times, taught him to read the water and the tides, to catch his own bait, to tie his own knots.

 As I will teach my daughter as well as soon as she is old enough. Already, however, she has caught a small Black-tip shark on her own and had her photo in the paper for a small Snook, which she caught. It shows her on the beach, giddy with glee, dancing on one foot, her windblown hair, covering one blue eye.

 The summer of 2005, Sky brought in 14 large Snook by himself, a Redfish, and five Spotted Sea Trout. I bought him an Inshore Slam T-shirt.

 We went fishing in Colorado on the Crystal River around Redstone, and he read the water so well, we caught 10 rainbow trout under a bubbling waterfall. When he was seven, he, his sister and I went out on the beach with our flashlights, well past midnight where we discovered a sea-turtle nest on the beach. We watched the hatchlings crawl out of their shells and swim away into the sea.

 We catch big black drum, 60 pounds or more, off the tip of the jetty on Pass-a-Grille. We go out and catch the fish beneath the full moon, fighting it down to the rocks to the beach. We bring it in and hear the boom, boom, boom, of the black drum.

 "Why do you think it makes that noise, dad?

 "I don't know, I think it may be a signal of some sort."

 Boom, boom, boom, it goes, with a slight bounce in it.

 My daughter's face wrinkles up, deep in thought. "Maybe it swallowed a drum," she says.

 I laugh and kiss her. Funny kid.

 The next day we play hooky and stay home, sleep in, something which we could never get away with in public school. One simply does not break the rules there. You come to school regularly and on time. Or they come and arrest you. Ha!

Sorry, but I'm not playing by their rules. Bit of a fishing bum, I am; I go with the tides.

I could not afford it, but when I considered my options I decided to send my kids to a private school in Gulfport, Florida: The Sunflower School. They handle his spirit with care, nurturing it, watering it and letting the sun in, so that he grows up straight and tall and beautiful, like a sunflower. I want a place that gives him their all.

They have 10-11 children per class, and a loving, caring teacher, who quite incidentally, loves to fish and has caught and landed a 150 pound Tarpon by herself. A large window, from floor to ceiling, allows sunlight to flood in, filling the children with cheer and delight.

They study science in a natural setting, and take walks to the beach to study fish, which they catch with their nets, then transfer to their school aquarium. They walk to the library in Gulfport and check out books, which they then read to the class. Each one has a library card, something which I believe is critical to spark a child's curiosity.

When they have completed their academic subjects for the day, they are not required to perform more mere busy work, answering repetitive workbook questions to pass another brainless test, they are free to wander the old wooden halls of the school and find a room where something of interest is always taking place.

Free to let their imaginations roam. And that's part of what fishing is about.

At Sunflower there's cooking classes, art and ceramic classes, music classes, marketing and business classes, where they learn to buy and sell their own crafts, or they can just sit in a corner window box and day-dream or read quietly to themselves.

It's something unique and exceptional, and I'm willing to give them my all so that they can have it, something almost lost in today's busy material world: childhood.

Then there's my daughter, Phoebe. An independent spirit, she attended public pre-school for one day and hated it. She did not wish to return, but wanted to stay with me on the beach and go fishing. She loves to fish. When I informed her little friends would miss her, she said, "Well, so what? I want to go fishing with you."

That's my girl.

So she stayed home with me. Swimming in the sea, fishing, biking, exploring, reading, writing. She's a happy little girl with bright, shining blue eyes and a take-charge attitude. One day, she will be a CEO, a lawyer or doctor, maybe even President of the United States, and I will be happy that I have given her everything I can.

It takes time and patience, things I've learned from fishing. There are days when I would rather be doing something else, but she and her brother come first.

They are not spoiled because I have not allowed it, but they are secure in the realization that their father loves them enough to cultivate a relationship with them above all else, when I could just as easily have sent them away for someone else to raise, a nanny, a teacher, a policeman, a prison. I am not, nor will I ever be, too busy for them. Instead of virtual reality in a video game, we go out – we test ourselves, not by pushing buttons on a video console, but by experiencing what real life has to offer.

They do not whine about life, they savor it.

Too many children are institutionalized at an early age. They don't know who their parents are, for it is always someone else with whom they spend their time. Consequently, the kids turn to video games, often violent, or to the vacuum of TV, sucking their lives into a fantasy world, played out against the backdrop of real life. They are living a virtual life, because a real one is not being offered to them.

Kids don't go fishing anymore, or satisfy their curiosity by learning from experience or a book, why would they when at the touch of a button, they blow someone's head off and score points for it? They are trophy children to put on the shelf when we are too busy, and sometimes I think it is our heads they would like to blow off.

I'm a good father and a good fisherman. Fatherhood is a big dream, one not left to others, so I honor my responsibility and take it seriously. I am raising my children.

I want to be the one who builds their character, and I want to indoctrinate the character of a fisherman into them.

Each night I catch a few trout, and take them home on a stringer. Now that I am divorced, when my children stay overnight, they help me clean and filet the fish before we eat them.

We chill them on ice, and sometimes stuff them with blue crab, which we also catch with a net down by the jetty, and a nice twice-baked potato. They have come to love the natural taste of seafood, and as a result, they are healthier, happier children.

I also changed my father's diet and have seen a dramatic improvement. He drinks only water and eats plenty of fruit and vegetables. He dines on the fresh fish I catch. His eyes have cleared and he has lost the dementia.

He began to sit up in bed. Some days, he even reads, which is promising because he was a Professor of English and books are the love of his life since his father, Harry Golden, was a famous Author; he has even started writing his own autobiography.

I tire of the flats of life and plead, beg and cajole my father into getting up out of bed.

I take him for long walks in his wheelchair on Pass-A-Grille; he can feel the wind and sun on his face. He has me stop as he turns to the west and raises his face to the sun.

Gradually he improves. His diabetes diminishes, then disappears altogether. His liver does not fail; he does not die. His cancer goes into remission, and he returns to his old self, although he cannot yet walk. He turns to his unfinished autobiography, AppleGate Autumn, which he publishes in the fall of 2004. His world is no longer flat.

He is inspired by my big dream of a big fish, and decides that he has a big dream of his own: to walk again. Big fish and inspiration go together it seems. No more little fish, this time, I'm giving my all. He will walk again!

I did learn one thing out there on the flats, however: not to settle for second best.

I want the best, and I am going to find a way to get it.

FEBRUARY, 2004. I hang around the docks at Merry Pier on 8th Avenue in Pass-A-Grille watching the fisherman catch trout. One in particular, is catching all the fish.

He is the one I want to talk to. He shows me how to use what he called a popper, an oblong, bright red or green bobber with beads attached to each end that makes a slurping noise, which trout find irresistible when you cast it into the water. You then whip it backwards so that it pops beneath a lure or live bait, a technique which drives trout absolutely crazy.

One particularly bleak and cloudy afternoon, with storm clouds riding the horizon, I return to the flats to try out my new popper.

My daughter is with me, and she sits down to watch. I wade out a little ways and cast out. As the popper hits the water, my rod is pointed out in front of me, as the trout fisherman instructed, parallel to the surface. Immediately, I flick the tip of my rod up and hear the distinctive pop—the bobber plunges and a speckled trout breaks the surface. A big one- 27 inches long.

What the Old Timers call a Gator Trout. The best of its species.

Two nearby fishermen, up to their knees in waders, also hook big trout, but lose them, when their adrenalin gets the better of them, and they attempt to horse them in. I hear them yelling and cursing, and I recall myself on the jetty where it all started, before I knew anything about fishing whatsoever.

However, having caught smaller trout all winter, I have learned how to reel in my line with a light, subtle touch because a trout's mouth, as delicate as paper, tears easily, and throws the hook. I bring the fish in slowly, putting the slightest pressure on it, leading it with the tip of my rod, backing off, giving it some slack when I have to, while bringing it ever closer to me.

I reel it up on the beach and the fishermen come running. They gaze at my fish in total disbelief.

"I didn't know they got this big," one says.

Even Phoebe, my daughter, not easily impressed, shouts—"Wow!" her eyes flashbulb bright. "You caught the biggest one, dad!"

"Yes," I beam. "I did."

"Look at that fish?" Exclaims one of the fisherman, genuine excitement in his voice.

"Is it really a trout?" Asks the other.

"Yes. A Gator trout," I hold it up proudly.

"What kind'a bobber is'zat?" The first fisherman asks.

"A popper." I answer, keenly aware that at last I know more than at least two other fisherman.

"Can I have some of your luck?" The second one wants to know.

I laugh, but it is the laugh of someone with a new-found confidence. It is a big speckled sea trout, one of the worthies in the fishing world. A Gator trout at that.

I whip out a tape measure I carry and measure the fish from jaw to tail. I take my time and stretch the tape way, way out for effect: 27 inches.

The other fisherman stare in awe, then walk quietly back to their spots and resume their stance, casting out in hopes that they too will catch a big fish. I remember the Old Salt's words about how luck can change from good to bad. Better to be prepared.

I toss out my popper again this time near the oyster bars—again as soon as it hits the water it ducks under and line plays out--fast. This time a Redfish slashes through the water. Again I have the second of my fish for an Inshore Slam – this time a 33 incher.

Again the fishermen come running over to see. They look at me like I am a voodoo child. That's two. Now I have to catch a Snook to claim the title of Inshore Slam. Nice to have problems.

But I'm not worried. It's my day.

I read a book called The Message of Water, about a man who talks to the water and photographs the beautiful crystals, which appear. According to him, water, the most mysterious and misunderstood element on earth, recognizes positive affirmation.

So before I toss my line out again, I hold my hand out and wave it over the water; I commend, honor and extol it for the life force that it holds within its watery depths.

"I love you, water," I extol. "I praise you and thank you for the fish that swim in your beautiful depths. I ask for a Snook."

The other fisherman look at me and shake their heads, but not for long.

I hook a jumbo shrimp beneath the popper and cast it up under the mangrove roots, ready for the best of the best. A sudden line-tightening intensity and it's on.

A Snook leaps out of the water. I reel it in and feel a swell of pride. Although it's a small Snook, 24 inches, it's a Snook at last.

My luck has changed. I've got an Inshore Slam.

I notice something else. Although they have been fishing in close proximity, the two other fishermen have not caught a single fish.

"Gotta get me one of them poppers," I hear them say as I release the Snook, pack up my tackle box and depart a happy man. I have made my dream of an Inshore Slam a reality.

I take my daughter's hand and we cross over to the island. I watch the other fisherman race to take my spot. I stand and observe them for a long moment. Still, they catch nothing, and I wonder why? Maybe there is such a thing as fisherman's luck after all. But I know differently. I was prepared today. Those who rely on luck, like professional gamblers, will tell you, it's more than luck. It's touch, feel, a sixth sense. Let it come to you, open yourself to it, and it will.

As we walk though the shadow of the pines, a large trout dangling on the end of my stringer, the discrepancy has not been lost on my daughter.

"Dad?"

"Yes, darling."

"Are you a great fisherman?"

"Not yet," I tell her honestly. "Catching the big trout this time really had more to do with luck than skill, but I'm learning how to wipe out the curse of the black spot.

"What?" she screws up her face, the freckles along the bridge of her nose, wrinkling.

"The Redfish has a black spot near its tail," I say. "It's an omen."

"Ome-" She winks one eye. "What's dat?"

"It's like a sign or something. Usually bad. To me it means halfway there, but not quite—maybe never. It means, the big Snook, that breaker of knots and hearts, is still out there."

"Oh," she says, considering. "But you caught three, and they didn't catch any. And they didn't have a popper like you."

"I know," I smile. "And maybe they didn't have something else."

"What?"

"They didn't have you."

She smiles and hugs me, and I know I am a lucky man indeed.

11 Dark Matter

Astrophysicists locate invisible objects, such as dark matter, interstellar clouds and black holes, by applying Einstein's gravitational theories to the geometry of spheres in motion. Visible objects react erratically, sometimes inexplicably, as their orbits become warped by invisible dark matter. Although undetectable to the naked eye, something is out there—something unseen which reveals itself only by association with actual observable phenomena. It is estimated that 90% of space is dark matter, and that we human beings are composed of star-stuff-the light of stars shining in our eyes.

So it was with the Shark Guy. He was composed of dark matter indeed. A black hole at the center, but you never saw it, for he revealed his true self only indirectly—by guesswork, examining the outward, visible appearance to ascertain the invisible.

Say what you will about him—he was psychotic perhaps-certainly certifiable- a Tiger Shark tattoo swimming up the length of his back, his top two canine teeth surgically removed, and replaced with shark's teeth fused into his jaw, a large Great White tooth worn around his neck like a trophy—but the Shark Guy was truly one of the very best shark fishermen in Shark-dom.

Short and stocky, yet powerfully built, he was always dressed in black. Black boots, black shirt and pants, worn childishly long, below his knees almost to his shins, which gave an air of utter ridiculousness, yet he was serious about sharks. His hair and his eyes were also black as night—no light of stars in those dark eyes.

He was obsessed with blood.

Black for black business.

I could always tell when he had been fishing from the jetty the night before. The next morning we would see a succession of decomposing shark heads wedged among the rocks. The jaws, having been pried loose, were missing. They looked like sad, gray deflated balloons. The bodies, he jettisoned over the side of the jetty, always without the dorsal fin. We would see their bodies, flensed white, underwater. A large pool of coagulated blood pooled on the jetty from the night's carnage.

When he did catch and land a large shark, he would beat it to death with a club, then blood-spattered as a butcher, saw their heads off with a hacksaw—slice the flesh from around the nose with a long, sharp filleting knife, stand on top of the head and pry out the jaws as a keepsake.

One time he caught a large black tip shark and dragged it along the jetty through the sand to the parking lot, leaving a long crimson trail of blood; roping the torso through the windows onto the roof of his old, rusted out black El Camino, he drove away down the street, the blood oozing down the sides onto the tires.

I believe the man was half-insane, but he knew how to catch and land the big ones, and this made him very interesting to me. His sole desire in life seemed to be to catch large sharks and wreak his vengeance upon the species. Why he is so obsessed with slaying and dismembering sharks, and with their blood, remains something of a mystery, but from what I observed, the man was extraordinarily complex.

He would arrive, with several of his beer-swilling buddies, and commandeer the jetty, setting up his poles at every station, north, south, east and west.

He would lash his rods and reels to the metal railings, surrounding the circumference of the jetty, then adjourn to swig a beer or two and swap fishing stories of the sharks he had caught.

For such a brutish, blood-soaked thug his stories were surprisingly poignant, evocative and eloquent, tinged with rare insight into the psyche of a flawed and imperfect human being. There was the one he told about rigging a large Bonita with a balloon to his 14 aut, then kayaking a mile out into the sea, to drop the bait far out beyond the buoys.

As he paddled back in to shore something grabbed the Bonita, his line snapped taught, whipping his face as his kayak spun around and headed relentlessly out to sea, carrying him out into the shipping lanes. He saw towering lights, he said, looming up out of the darkness, as wide as a city block and high as a sky-scrapper.

He did not know if what he was seeing was the incoming lights of one ship or two—but they were coming straight at him, his tiny kayak all but invisible. It was either take his chances or do the prudent thing and cut the shark loose. He chose to take his chances, navigating inside the lanes, down the middle, between two large ocean freighters, while tethered to a Tiger Shark. He finally landed the shark- a monster 8 foot 11 inch foot Tiger shark, whose jaws, he smiled, and his golden shark teeth flashed—hung on his living-room wall.

Often, he and his friends would fish by the light of a single lantern late into the night. I know, because whenever he fished there, I would creep out and watch him, compelled by some inner alien demon of curiosity, which I could neither comprehend nor fight.

One night, a huge shark head, decapitated from its body, lay in a pool of its own blood in the middle of the jetty. Its jaws were still intact. I approached it and nudged it with my big toe--wham!

Its jaws clamped down—narrowly missing my toe—locked shut. It had been dead for nearly an hour, and still its unrelenting jaws retained the ability to snap down involuntarily, locking its teeth in a deadly vise-like grip. No wonder they have never gone extinct after hundreds of millions of years.

Often the Shark Guy would lay out chum, right off the jetty, next to the beach on Pass-A-Grille.

When I tried to point out that Pass-a-Grille is a family beach for swimmers, he scoffed. "Shark-bait!" Sort of a half, mocking snort, half-curse, though most everything had a bit of a curse added on. Their safety never occurred to him.

Once that summer a swimmer was bitten by a small shark in broad daylight, and taken to the hospital-- an uncommon occurrence. I remember wondering if it had anything to do with Shark Guy drawing them in close. I think in the end someone complained, and the police chased him away, because after that summer, I never saw him again. Although I must confess, it was awfully boring without him.

Once, well past midnight in late June, my kids and I crept out to see if he had caught anything. To our astonishment a gigantic sting ray blocked our path. Ten feet from wing-tip to wingtip we had to hug the railing, to step around it because it covered the entire entrance to the jetty.

The Shark Guy cut off its tail, sliced its fins to make it bleed, then hooked it as he and his buddies shoved it back off the jetty to use as bait.

It was an awesome sight as it swam away into the dark water, wings aflutter, sending the scent of blood out into the deep, dark places where the monsters swim, with each stroke.

We waited for what seemed like hours to see what would happen until finally my kids fell asleep on the bench beside me, and I began to doze off when a curse like a cannon shot went off in my ear.

"Fish on-you bastard!" He screamed.

Out beyond the buoys, a gigantic shark leapt from the dark waves. It must've been at least 12 feet long. It was hooked, the giant ray in its mouth.

The Shark Guy climbed up on the railing and raged at the beast. Roaring, laughing, cursing-- he reeled it in, pumping fast and furious, like an insane hurdy gurdy organ grinder to a dissonant demonic music, which he alone could hear.

He leapt backwards off the rail and landed on a sail-cat he had caught earlier that evening, and inadvertently cast aside, the nail-sharp dorsal fin sticking through the sole of his boot.

"Blood!" He screamed in rage. His minions knelt to unlace his boot. His sock was blood-drenched. Hobbling around on one foot, he left a bloody trail of footprints in his wake.

"Chum!" He chortled and I shuddered, wondering what kind of devil's bargain he had made to catch these great sharks. That was all he fished for, obsessively night after night, the summer of 2005. Furthermore, it was his blood he was using as chum.

Every once in a while he would take a swig of beer and reel in more line. As he dragged the shark close to the jagged rocks, everyone ran to the edge to see.

The shark still held the giant stingray lodged in its mouth, half in half out and was busily chewing on it. It had dislodged the hook, but it would not let go of the sting-ray. What was worse, the Sting Ray was still flapping in its jaws.

Shark Guy leaned way over the rail and attempted to gaff the shark, even as his more prudent buddies tried to warn him it was no longer hooked. When he did gaff it—just inside the jaw, the shark dropped the ray, thrashed it tail and spun away, pulling the Shark Guy over the railing into the water with it.

I heard his muffled curses, curiously muted underwater.

But his predicament did not seem to bother him in the least. He laughed as he rode the water like a skier, bouncing up and down across the waves. Incredibly he was still hanging onto the end of the gaff as the shark towed him around the south side of the jetty.

We ran to the southern rail just as he flew by. "Let go!" His drunken buddies urged him on.

He cursed the beast up one side and down the other. The shark turned and headed back the other way.

"Turn away, kids." I said, scooping them into my arms. "We're going home." There was going to be blood in the water, and I didn't want them to see.

So of course they slipped beneath my arms and raced to the railing to watch the Shark Guy being dragged out to sea by the biggest shark I have ever seen. But I noticed he was not holding onto the gaff any longer—he was holding onto the dorsal, riding the wake of the shark.

It was then that I realized I was dealing with something invisible inside the man. Something which motivated him, which neither I nor his buddies could see. The hidden motives, the secret dreams and delusions—the dark matter of the human heart.

When he was almost out to the buoys, and lost to the darkness, he let go and swam nonchalantly back to the jetty as if he were swimming laps in a pool.

He climbed up out of the water onto the rocks, dripping wet and sauntered drunkenly along the jetty, sloshing along, one boot on one boot off.

"Damn!" He swore. "That was fun!"

12 "Fear Itself": Lesson Of The Shark

It was every parent's worst nightmare. The children were in the water snorkeling. I was wading near the shore—when I beheld the shadow. Even from a distance I knew what it was. Seven to eight feet long, unbearably dark, it swam parallel to shore, its dorsal fin slicing through the clear green water. And it was closing in fast.

The effect was mesmeric, sunlight and shadow, in a dappled dance of death, a shifting effervescent underwater kaleidoscope of beauty and destruction.

I could not take my eyes off it!

Trying not to panic, I shouted at my daughter, gesturing wildly for her to swim to me. She turned her head, looked right at the large dorsal fin swimming in her direction and took off as fast as her little legs could carry her. The shark glided by.

When she finally reached the shore and the safety of my arms, I swept her up and showered her with kisses, my heart pounding in my ears.

It was my son I was worried about. Further out, snorkeling near the rocks on the northern boundary of the jetty, he was underwater and oblivious to my cries of warning. When he resurfaced—it was too late. He was stuck between the shark and the shore.

"Don't move!" I commanded, and he obeyed. As a predator the shark is equipped with extraordinary sensory input; it can detect even the slightest movement, as subtle as a ripple, with uncanny accuracy.

The White Tip, an ocean shark, has been known to track its prey, the unwary shipwreck survivor, or unlucky diver, kicking to stay afloat in blue water, by following the path of their vibrations through the water, across a vast wide sea, from a distance of a mile or more.

Swimming deliberately, the shark glided gracefully through the crystal-clear, waist deep water about ten yards from the sandbar, between where my son now stood and the shore. Its dorsal cut the surface of the shallow green water like a cruising submarine, the length of its body partially submerged a dark looming presence.

I remember every detail: the look of primal fear, along with the dawning recognition, etched on my son Skyler's freckled face as the shark slides past. He stands absolutely still, only his eyes moving as he follows the trajectory of the shark's forward progress. As the fin sweeps by, all that is visible of the palpable threat that swims below the surface, I hold my breath and glance into my son's eyes, trying to hide my fear lest he panic. We are playing a waiting game, each of us, standing perfectly still, praying the fin does not turn.

There is nothing I can do. I feel sick inside. Helpless. As it glides by, in front of our eyes, I peer beneath the surface to see what kind of shark we're dealing with—Bull Shark, extremely dangerous and unpredictable—a man eater. And it's swimming mere yards from my son.

It takes forever to swim by.

It continues its leisurely pace towards the jetty.

As it passes by, my son, very calmly at first, then with mounting speed, walked off the sandbar, waded quietly through the waist-deep water, then raced through the shallow water, the last few yards to shore. I hugged him tightly, holding onto him **as** if I would never let him go. His sister, for once, is happy to see him as well, basking in the pleasure of his company.

But it is not over. Yet. The three of us follow the big Bull down the shore, racing him to the jetty. Running ahead, Skyler jumps onto a rocky ledge to more closely observe its coming approach.

It is heading directly for him, when it senses the structure of the jetty directly in front of it—with an insouciant flick of its scythe-like tail, it slashes due west—toward the open sea, dips its pectoral fins---and dives like a stealth bomber, wearing the underwater shadows like a cloak of invisibility.

It utterly vanishes before our eyes. A shadow among shadows.

I stand a long time and gaze at the open water. I recall those times my children and I have leapt off the jetty into the water, to dive among the schools of fish down by the rocks, and search for conchs, and, although it's been a year since he's been around, I remember The Shark Guy. Although it is relatively shallow just off the tip of the jetty, and normally quite clear, out beyond the buoys it is bordered by a deep, dark void of fathomless blue shadows, out of which, in fact, I've always thought anything might emerge, and into which an eight foot Bull shark has just sashayed as if it were part of the shadows itself. Now as I dive down for Conch on the bottom, as I reach to grab the shells, I keep one eye on the darkness further out, and I stay between the shadows and my children.

Never since have I ventured into the Gulf, that I do not maintain a constant vigil on the surrounding water. Weed lines, casting an undulating shadow, unnerve me. Schools of baitfish send a shiver up my spine as they glide as one, a large silver apparition beneath the contours of the sea.

Try as I might, I cannot seem to shake the memory of that day—of how close the jaws of death brushed by. It has left a scar. And a lesson to be learned. The lesson of the shark. Primal fear!. There are dark and dangerous aspects to life and to fishing. Everything is not as it appears to be. The sun may be shining, the sky blue, the water sparkling, yet still there are things out there—wild, untamed things under and on the water, which a fisherman will, if he continues long enough, have to come to terms with. Stormy seas, waves breaking over the bow, cancer and disease- marine engines that breakdown too far from shore – evil that roams the earth. And sharks with rows of teeth that regenerate as soon as they fall out. I have seen their jaws up close- they are killing machines. A healthy respect, a large hook, and a steel leader, is a good thing to remember when going shark fishing. And never forget to bring a gaff.

I made a vow. To reclaim my immaculate love of the sea, to allay the irrational fear in my heart, I will catch a shark, as large or larger than the one that day, and mount its jaws, like the shark guy, on my living room wall.

At first I thought I'd have to go down to Key West, but The Shark Guy, informed me that there were many very big sharks right off the jetty at night. A fact I can confirm first hand. In the end, all I had to do was cross the street.

MIDNIGHT: SUMMER 2006. To that end I have come to the jetty tonight, to face my fears and catch the shadow that lurks, like I know the sun rises and sets, out there beyond the buoys.

The clicker on my 006 reel is set. I have sent a balloon out into the channel, above a hook as large as my hand, baited with a fresh cut Bonita. I have an eight and a half foot 150 pound steel leader and 700 yards of 80 pound braid.

It's late and lonely as hell out here, but I wait by the light of a single lantern.

Then I feel the first tantalizing touch.

Click.

I leap to the railing as the tip of my rod quivers, then lays still. Deep down something big is circling. It's testing my bait, bumping it, teasing it.

Click, click...

I grab the rod and tighten the star drag a bit, waiting for the next—

Click! And then it bites hard. My line snaps taught and begins to race out of the spool, the drag wailing in the moonlight, not singing beautifully as usual, but screaming maliciously, like a lost soul in freefall.

So this is what catching a shark is like. I hold on and let it run. It's all I can do.

I'm getting spooled. 100—200-300-450-550-600-all 700 yards. It's going out fast. My stout Star Rod is bent double, to the breaking point. I'm afraid it's going to shatter into a thousand pieces, and splinter in my face. It's a real concern. I want to cover my eyes, just in case, but I need two hands to hold on tight.

The tip of the rod is being driven deep into my gut and the weight of the shark has wrenched my back out. My eyeballs feel like they're going to pop out of my skull.

The shark is pulling with such power, I swear it's going to wrench the jetty off its foundation, yank the bedrock right out from under my feet and tow us out to sea with it. My braid is all but gone, I'm down to the mono backing when it comes up—an enormous shark, gray as a shadow in the moonlight, leaps from the waves.

It's a monster. I pump and reel in fast and furiously, fighting it around the southern extremity of the jetty, running down along the slippery, uneven rocks, gaining line an inch at a time, slowly bringing the beast to me. I jump off the rocks at a run and down the shore, hearing the metal reel groan, bend and slip as the shark is brought to bear. For a moment I'm afraid the reel's going to disintegrate in my hands.

    I screw down the drag even tighter and heave back with all my weight—if the line snaps--it snaps. I'm going to fight it with all I've got. Surprisingly, I feel it give. The shark swings around and heads straight for the jetty. I can see its fin cutting a swath through the water in the moonlight. I feel a tingle run up my spine.

    It's big and dark and coming straight at me, like something out of Jaws. I can almost hear the soundtrack—the devil sawing on his cello in the lower register. Doom, doom, doom, doom… Or is that my heartbeat?

    Takes me a moment to realize I'm up to my knees in the surf. In the excitement I'd forgotten I had gone into the water. Although I cannot tell what kind of shark it is, from where I stand it looks too big, maybe ten feet long, as if a hurricane had dredged up an ancient shipwrecked galleon and blew it towards shore.

    I want to throw down my rod and reel and run. But I don't! I hold on in this brawl with the monster, struggling with myself as much as the shark, with pain and loss, with fear itself---and slowly I am winning.

    I watch it thrash near shore, half in, half out of the water, its dark dorsal straight up like a deadly blade. I reel in line and circle it cautiously, noting it has swallowed almost all my eight foot steel leader. Its malignant little eyes regard me indifferently, a sneer on its lips. It lashes its tail, like a bully, and shoots a spray of salt-water in my face.

    Stealthily, I unsheathe my knife. I will take my trophy now. I recall that day on the beach when we walked in its shadow, and I want those jaws on my mantle.

Then I remember with sadness the great Hammerhead, taken in Boca Grande, pregnant with young. Killed for a fisherman's pride. From its great girth, this shark too, looks like it may be pregnant. And therein lies the second lesson of the shark: Grace. I am not a killer, just a fisherman using my instincts. As is he. It's the law of nature to be what he is. Who am I to judge? It is I, in fact, who, if I chose to take its life, would be the cold-blooded killer.

I decide to let it go. Before I release it, however, I will draw first blood. I reach out and slash it once across the upraised dorsal, just to let it know I have won. I cut the braided line and it spins free, thrashing and slashing into deeper water before it turns, like a battleship and swims slowly out of sight.

It will carry my mark on its dorsal, as I carry the scar of my encounter with the jaws of death in my heart. Third lesson of the shark: This night I have fought and defeated you—O Death, and I am no longer afraid. There is only one way to conquer yout fears: face them.

13 "Sea School": Lesson Of The Hammerhead

October, 2005, I visited the Keys with my son to attend sea camp at the Newfound Harbor Marine Institute. A few miles beyond Marathon, on Big Pine Key, the institute is billed as a unique educational adventure where kids can "discover the wonders of the realms beneath the sea." Kids sleep in dorms, arise early and attend class by exploring wild mangrove islands and coral reefs, learning about coastal ecology, not from the pages of a text book, but diving and snorkeling in the living sea.

When they find a specimen, down among the coral reefs, they bring it up to the surface and hold class on the spot aboard an oceanographic research vessel, known as a flattop.

In this school the blackboard is the deck of the flattop.

My son dove in and soon reappeared holding a sponge with a small crustacean inside. The instructor shook the sponge and a blue crab scuttled across the deck, its claws aloft. She scrawled its scientific designation across the deck of the flattop with a piece of chalk, then proceeded to discuss the specimen with the children.

There was not a bored or uninterested face in the crowd.

As the kids splashed and swam, my eyes strayed toward the waters. One look told me all I need to know. High outgoing tide. Birds and baitfish.

I drive to the bridge on Islamorada, where the water is so clear and blue it hurts the eyes. Because fish love structure, I know the fishing will be good around that bridge.

I take down my rented kayak and drop it into the water off the side of the bridge. I paddle further out, drop a Sabiki and reel in several pin-fish.

I look down to see a dark, looming shadow hiding beneath my little water-craft.

A shark, almost as large as the Kayak itself, is waiting beneath my boat to ambush a Tarpon. Once hooked, the prey will not be able to escape. Sharks are smart. And crafty. They wait for me to catch them dinner.

I weigh my options. I can call it quits and paddle away now or take my chances. The adrenalin is pumping. I can't quit. I've come to catch a Tarpon, so I cast out a live pin-fish—Wham! Instant hookup! A silver King leaps from the water, suspended against the high white clouds, then crashes in free-fall, sideways in a mountainous spray.

And then the shark is on it. I look beneath my Kayak. The shark has vanished, but I know where it's going; I watch a dark shadow swim, like a ravenous sea-wolf, straight toward its intended prey, now lashed to my line like a sacrificial goat staked to a leash.

It is a sea of shadows. Beneath crystalline waters, the beauty nearly comparable to the destruction. The Kayak spins 180% and careens off- hooked to a bolt of silver blue; the Tarpon leaps from the water ahead of me, the sharks closing in for the kill.

I lean back and set the hook hard, five or six times, to drive the point into the Tarpon's tough sinewy jaw. Each time it leaps, I lean forward in what's known as "the bow."

Three thoughts come to mind: 1). I have jumped a Tarpon; 2). In a kayak; 3).In shark-infested waters. And a fourth creeps in unbidden. I do not like sharks. They spook me—bad!

The line is spooling out fast. The Tarpon is running for its life, heading for the pylons around the bridge. In all my dreams of big fish, it was never like this.

This is serious, trouble on every side. A nightmare set in water. But I do have the biggest fish I've ever hooked on the end of my line; I have to look at it just to make sure it's real.

It did not take long for the first dorsal fin to show. A big Hammerhead, coming up out of nowhere-fast. Probably the one hiding under my boat.

It hits with such force it shakes my little kayak, dips its bow beneath the surface, then spins it around like a top. Fortunately, the shark became snagged, caught up in the line as it twisted and turned, rolling over and over, teeth flashing, tail thrashing, the terrified Tarpon clasped in its unrelenting vise-like grip. The big Hammerhead clamped down hard and bit the Tarpon in half, a dark red cloud dissipating in the water.

I sit back in shock. My dream lies scattered in pieces, ravaged by the shark, silver tarpon scales floating dirge-like on the sea.

Other fins appear. They slashed and tore at the bobbing underbelly, gorging on the other half of the fish in a frothing cauldron of blood and streaming entrails. A feeding frenzy as sharks consumed every trace of that Tarpon, till there was nothing left but the head, decapitated, its large eyes staring into space.

I reeled in the Tarpon's head, still stuck on my hook, re-rigged, using 100 pound steel leader, and cast out again. My rod bent double, the drag screaming. I had hooked the big hammerhead, and the fight was on. As I pumped and reeled the shark closer to my boat, the great big hammerhead got hammered by something even bigger.

The back-lash of sea-spray left in its wake, told me all I needed to know.

The steel leader, as taught as a violin string, snapped like the crack of a whipcord, whistling through the air, as I watched the big Hammerhead being devoured as it had only moments before, devoured. It was carried away in the jaws of something massive, enormous. Big does not begin to describe it. As large and wide as a Volkswagen Van. Without the peace sign in the window.

As I fought the hammerhead--I felt another tug, this time smaller, yet still strong.

There were hundreds of smaller sharks in the water in a feeding frenzy. I watched as the big one got a chunk bitten out of its torso, then in a cloud of blood, turned and devoured a piece of its own flensed body flesh.

And me without a gaff. And this is one of the lessons: never go shark fishing without a gaff!

This was Hammerhead Lesson written in blood. For the big fights in life, you had better be prepared. Prepared to fight and maybe lose, but not to allow defeat to overcome and overwhelm you. Today, in this fight I was trounced, no doubt about it, but I will come back to fight another day, and this time I will come prepared. I'll be back, fish! And I will bring my gaff.

Later, on the way home, we will stop and fish off a jetty; my son Sky will catch two small sharks: a Bonnethead and a Blackfin. We freeze them and he takes them to his science class to dissect them. The younger kids are in awe. It's like they too get to have class right on the deck of a flattop and witness the wonders of nature close up.

When I arrive to pick him up later that day I see a little kid run to his mother and say. "Mom, school was so cool today. I got to hold a shark's heart in my hand."

That's the way I feel. I held a shark in my hand, pulled fresh from the sea, and it was way cool. Science class on the deck of a boat. Shark 101. "You see, class, sharks are predators and…" Until you've been there, in the midst of it, class is over for today.

I have a recurring dream: In my dream several dark fins are swimming towards me, all submerging just before they reach my Kayak.

I feel the water moving beneath me; It's unstable, and I'm sinking as I watch them plunge under my boat, mere inches from my feet, my heart pounding, echoing in the silence of my dream, and then the big hammerhead moves in and I awake and tell myself it was only a dream. But I know it wasn't; for I have, to quote Shakespeare seen, "the green sea incarnadined" before my eyes, and I cannot forget. For I myself, have been to sea-school, and a big Hammerhead was my Masters and my PhD.

14 The Turning Of The Tide: Lesson Of The Tides

MAY 1st: 2004: SUNSET. On the Jetty. Purple dusk. I'm using an artificial tonight, a 12 inch top-water, bomber, red and white, casting it just beyond the sunken rocks and retrieving it fast. I'm bearing two poles with two different types of reels and line: One, a 7' foot Shimano, Saragosa, with a line weight of 12-20 pounds, medium action, strung with 30 pound power pro braided line, tied to a 20 pound fluorocarbon leader is for big fish, the other, a custom-built fast-action Tornado, 8-12 pound weight, strung with 20 pound test, and knotted with a loop knot, is for lures to catch live bait. I always bring two rigs now. One to catch the bait, the other to catch the big fish. I know the Snook are here, and I know where they school. By the rocks, where I snagged the first one. Most people do not realize what is right under their noses--and I don't tell them unless they ask.

My giant, three tiered tackle-box is crammed full of every conceivable kind of lure and artificial. I'm still having trouble with knots, however, and am not as confident as I appear when I stride up with an arm full of rods and tackle and set to work.

On my first cast with the bomber I get lucky. A Ladyfish smashes into the lure. The Tornado rod bends double, and the fish skyrockets in a bolt of blue, splashing from the water, in a dazzling aerial display, that I know is more show than anything.

Having caught dozens of them out on the flats, I know it's an easy fish to land, yet I play it for all its worth, pulling it up to make it jump again and again, all the way to the jetty, to a crowd of cheering onlookers.

No one else has caught anything yet. I just walked up, cast in and pulled in a big Ladyfish on the first cast, so I look like I'm the man tonight, but I know better.

I just made it look easy. The hard part, I know is coming, for I know big Snook take to Ladyfish like candy, and now I've got to produce the real thing.

Fortunately, it is high tide, and the currents are ripping past us. I have learned not to even bother fishing for Snook unless the tides are right. Otherwise it is a waste of time.

The crowd parts when I bring the fish up on the jetty, land him, grab my big fish rig and hook the Lady through the dorsal. Measured, it is 24 inches or two feet.

"What are you doing," a tourist asks incredulously.

"Bait," I say with a grin, enjoying the effect it has on the crowd. Their looks say if that's your bait, what is the fish you're fishing for?

I climb down onto the rocks, searching the rocks.

"I'd be happy just to catch that fish," a fisherman on the jetty speculates.

Not me. I want more than bait this time; I cast out again along the rocks to the south, open my bail and let the Ladyfish drift in the current. It does not take long! Yet even I'm surprised by the incredible belligerence of the bite.

Fish On!

My bail begins to scream as the line runs out- fast. I look down at the rocks, but the fish—a giant Snook is already leaping out of the water, twenty yards off the north end of the jetty.

Up on the jetty, the fishermen crane their necks around, eyes wide. By the expression on their faces, they must be fishermen of small fish, for I don't think they've quite heard that sound before. It's the sweetest sound there is.

"What the –"

His words are cut short as the giant Snook rises up in front of him, leaping out of the water at the end of the jetty.

It's happened too fast. I hooked the Snook in the rocks in front of me, now he's twenty yards away in the time it took me to turn my head to the west. I race up the rocks, rod in hand just in time to watch it rise up, up, up, thick, heavy, black-striped, a golden Snook of mammoth proportions as wide as it is long. 40-45 inches. The dream become flesh. This is what I've been waiting for.

Wait, and the tide will turn. Wait and your dream will come true. That is the lesson of the tides. Timing is everything

"Damn!" I husk, my mouth gone dry. There's no time to think or react. Instinct kicks in and I know I'm in for a brawl, a knock down drag out fight. I'm stunned by its sheer size and power. It slices the Ladyfish in half and consumes the part with the hook, diving deep, the line sizzling off the reel, driving my heavy pole down, so I have to fight to keep it up.

"Jesus! It's a Snook! Biggest one I've ever seen." Someone says.

And it's on the end of my line. It's been two years now, since I hooked my first one, and then another six months on the flats since I got my slam.

I've got 30 pound test on the reel, so I'm not worried, but my heart is pounding against my chest, and the adrenalin's pumping so hard I'm shaking.

The crowd is hushed as I fight the fish to a standstill, pull it away from almost certain entanglement with the crab-trap, which the Old Salt has warned me about, lug it around the westernmost projection of the jetty, and fight it down along the northern side of the pillar of rocks towards the shore.

To keep up with it, I am forced to sprint along the rocks, slipping, falling, rising once again with bruised knees and a bloody elbow, my line flying out faster than I can reel it back in, but I've got 250 yards of line on the spool, so I'm confident, yet the incredible acceleration of the fish is such that I have to back off and let him run back out again because my line's so taught it's ready to snap.

I fight the urge to let him run. The last time I did that I lost the fish. I want him so bad; I stand there bleeding and cursing and laughing at the same time. This fish is mine.

Time is suspended as I fight the fish of my dreams, the crowd looking on, following my every move, and then the unthinkable happens. A sharp retort rings in my ears and my line flies back over my head. My knot had broken again!

There is an audible sigh when the air goes out of a crowd, which sounds like someone getting sucker punched in the gut. "Awwwhhh."

"He lost it!" someone cries.

"I can't believe it," wails another.

Grimly I gather my belongings, blood trickling down my arm, and stalk away into the shadows. Not a word is spoken as I pass.

When I get home I have a message on my cell-phone. My divorce was final and the destruction is complete. I suddenly miss my children. An ache deep in my gut. I have not seen them for over a week. My heart is heavy, numb with loss.

After dinner, as I prepare for bed, as I brush my teeth I look at myself in the mirror and I break down; I got down on my knees and wept. A cry of love. A cry of lost and broken dreams. I wept till there were no more tears. It seemed as if, no matter how hard I tried, all my big dreams were destined to never come true.

The wasted years of writing, teaching, of parenting of being a care-giver; it all seemed connected to fishing, all seemed to have been lost with the big Snook. I had lost everything. Because I had still not learned to tie a proper knot, and once loosed, the knot had slipped, and with it everything I had loved.

Irretrievably it seemed the ties that bind were broken. I had grown over-confident. I had caught a Gator Trout, a Big Red and a small Snook with my simple overhand knot, and in my pride, I thought it was enough. But it was not enough.

Not enough to hold a big fish or land the big dream.

When I rose up off my knees, I vowed to do whatever it took this time to catch and land a big one, to fish on in spite of it all. The tide had turned. I knew I would never give up now. For me, the tides would turn again. And I had learned something else. When to fish the tides. Low, incoming for the mangroves, high, outgoing for the jetty and the beaches. Or, if you really want to get in on the action, at the turning of the tides. But first I would have to learn to tie a little knot.

15 Of Knots, The Ties That Bind

Everything begins and ends with a knot. The importance of knots, in fishing as in life, should not be underestimated. It is a delicate maneuver, to tie a knot correctly and make it close tight, to hold even the biggest fish. It requires patience, practice and skill, virtues, which fishing teaches well.

Knots are the very foundation of our lives; if not tied correctly, relationships founder, marriages crumble, business partnerships split up, and death, that great un-raveller of all knots, slips its hangman's noose about our throat.

When I fish I use three knots. Just three knots. These comprise my repertoire. With them I possess the confidence to pursue big dreams and big fish. If the knot holds I will catch my fish and land my dream, if it breaks, I lose everything, so I tie them with care.

Knots are the weakest link in connecting us to our dream, critical to our success or failure in fishing and in life. I don't know why I waited until so long, laziness perhaps, or inertia, not being able to make the first move; maybe I just instinctively knew it was my weakness and did not want to deal with the issue.

Whatever the cause, I paid the price. I lost a lot of big fish before I caught one.

I was uninitiated in the practical applications of knot tying. It seemed too complicated, the intricacies of a knot, and something which I could never master. A bit of a klutz, my fine motor skills are somewhat suspect, so it was physically awkward for me.

To me all knots seemed to border on the realm of the metaphysical, a type of medieval alchemy. My fingers fumbled with even the simplest knot.

How then, I reasoned, was I going to learn to tie a more complex knot than the one I had always used? I knew the answer – the Snook had told me.

I was used to catching little fish, and to catch and land them, a simple, uncomplicated knot was adequate, but the big fish required a stronger more reliable knot to hold them fast. Therefore, I knew I had to learn this incomprehensible skill—not to try was not an option.

I bought several types of line on which to practice: braid, monofilament, and fluorocarbon, each having its strength and weaknesses. I soon discovered that monofilament, the most inexpensive and popular type of line, has a tendency to slip when the knot is tied to something other than the line itself, and when tied in conjunction with certain knots at particular angles, will self-cut if a big fish puts pressure on it.

Again I tried such knots as the Figure Eight, the half-hitch and the double half-hitch, but they sometimes self-cut back upon themselves, and therefore, they were to be avoided when using monofilament.

The next line I tested was fluorocarbon, an excellent line for Snook and other wary predators since it becomes almost invisible underwater. The more proficient I become, the more I prefer the use of fluorocarbon, especially for leaders and free-lining, although much of it is up to individual taste and personal opinion.

In my opinion, a 36-44 inch fluorocarbon leader will out-fish, outperform and out-catch all other fishing leaders. It works like magic.

Put two fishermen side by side: one is using mono, the other fluoro; the one with the fluoro will inevitably catch the fish. I know this from experience. I've seen it, time and time again, with my own eyes.

For instance, once there was a little girl down on the cove near Land's End. She was out-fishing us all. I thought she must be incredibly lucky, until I delved a little deeper. I asked her what she was using. 20 pound fluorocarbon, 10 pound braid, was her answer. Her father had set her up. He nodded at me with a knowing glance. Then I understood it was not so much a hot hand, as a light leader. Luck had nothing to do with it. This practical application solved the issue for me once and for all. Up until that time I had been using 30 pound mono; I switched to a lighter fluoro and the results have been all the proof I require.

For the main line, braid, as the Old Salt had predicted, quickly became my favorite all around line. Extremely versatile and easy to tie, weather to a leader, a hook, or line to line, braid is thin yet strong, providing the angler with hundreds of yards of extra line on the spool, of a greater pound test.

When spooled, the reel will hold three to four times more braided line than either mono or fluorocarbon, and it will cast longer and reel in faster. A distinct advantage when using a top-water lure to catch a fishes's eyes, or when the fish is a wary species, like the Snook.

Braid comes in a variety of colors, so, if an angler chooses bright yellow for instance, he can watch it play out through the water as a fish begins its run, making it easier to determine the exact moment when the line becomes taught enough to set the hook.

Red is a good color since it becomes invisible at depth underwater. The new white crystal fire line is interesting, but the new Daiwa Samurai line, light and strong, and eminently cast able, is by far the best I've found yet.

Since setting the hook is the key to landing a big fish, knowing where your line is at all times increases the odds in your favor. When hooking a fish, especially a large one, split-second timing is crucial. Set the hook too early and you lose him, too late and he steals your bait and you get "smoked like a cheap cigar."

There are three stages to catching a big fish: Setting the hook, reeling the fish in and landing it. Each requires its own technique. A lot of over anxious anglers try and set the hook the moment they feel the bite, or when sight-casting, set the hook the moment the fish takes the bait. Their line comes up empty every time.

With a little patience they might have caught the big one.

To set the hook properly, resist your first impulse to yank back when you feel the bite, or when the fish begins its initial run; allow your line to play out in a steady acceleration until it's almost stretched tight, then just before the moment it snaps taut, snap it lightly with a flick of the wrist.

If the line stops going out, or slackens momentarily, don't snap back yet — it means the fish has paused to further nibble the bait, spit it out, or may be circling for another strike.

It takes great discipline to wait and see if the fish has swum away or if it will return. Most people will reel in, and lose an opportunity for a second chance.

Sometimes, with the bigger fish, they strike -- and they're on; you don't have to wait, but the hook has not gone deep enough to stay in. It's best to use caution when setting the hook.

Fish On!

When you do set your hook correctly, you will feel the big fish and the action intensify immediately. He will run with it. The big fish knows it's hooked. The drag will begin to sing. An explosion may occur on top of the water, if it's a Snook or Tarpon, as it jumps and tries to throw the hook.

Keep the line firm and taut, but do not "horse it," pull or yank your line back in, or you pull the bait and the hook out of its mouth. Wait- learn patience, go by touch, you will know when.

Once hooked, apply steady pressure on the fish, reeling back in as much line as you can get, but if it begins to run, and take your line, let it. That's part of the fun of fighting a big fish—the give and take. When it tires and you feel a pause in the action, reel back in some line.

An excellent strategy for tiring a big fish is to fish it "down and dirty," that is to turn your rod sideways to try and flip him and break his spirit. If you can make it fight against the tide. This will tire him more quickly. When the line snaps taut and you feel it turn and run with the tide, let it run out again or it may break you off, then begin all over again, until slowly, but surely, you are pumping and reeling in more line than is going out.

At this stage, allow a big fish to run in any direction it desires, giving it as much head as he requires, unless it's running toward the rocks, the mangroves, or a pier or piling. Then you have to turn it. To do this you will need a good stout rod with backbone and a lot of nerve. Personally, instead of fighting him in too quickly in that first sweet rush of adrenalin, I like I play him, to lead him with the tip of the rod, in the give and take of a tug of war with a big fish on. I bring him in slowly, almost without him knowing, then at the end, finish him off down and dirty, and watch as he comes in as docile as a lamb.

I like to take my time as I always learn something about a fish that way. To see how it fights. When it is ready to give up, it will swim right into your hands. When it is, simply bow down and receive it—all fight gone. Easy.

With a few exceptions. I once asked the Shark Guy a question.

"Do big sharks tire out like other fish," I asked him. "Then come in easy?"

"Let's put it this way," he giggled, an eerie sensation with those Tiger Shark teeth implants. "If I catch the right kind of shark, I'll be here all night and all the next day, and possibly the following night. I'll be tired, but he will still be fighting."

Snook, Redfish and Trout, however, as well as most other fish, will, when fished correctly quickly tire and dog it. All you have to do is reel them in and scoop them up into your hand or net.

One more important thing to remember. The adrenalin rush—adrenalin, a natural substance within the body triggered by stress, will start ripping through you like a fire. It can flare up suddenly out of control, speed up your heart-rate up, and make you do stupid things; it is also the cause of more lost fish than anything else.

When you are hooked to a big one, and your entire body, shaking, your muscles aching, and your heart feels like it's about to burst, when your eyes are going dim and your throat is tight and dry, relax. Fight to remain calm and steady- unflustered. Remember to breathe. Stay composed. Fight that fish. Keep your wits about you or the fish will beat you every time.

Endure, be patient, disciplined and stand and fight. Do it wisely with a strategy. As long as the big fish or the big dream is on the other end of the line, you have a chance of pulling it in, so don't give up before the fight is over.

It's important to maintain a positive attitude, not to allow those negative thoughts into your head.

In times of stress like these, a little hair-line fracture (or larger) in your psyche will open a pathway to your brain, and you may hear a flood of negative voices: I'll never amount to anything, I can't do it, I'm a loser. Don't listen. This fish, this dream is yours if you keep your cool and fish on.

There are stages to every fight: setting the hook, letting the fish run, playing the fish until you land it. To properly set the hook, you must wait until the slack in line is out—you will see your line stretch taught, just before it does-set hook; from there, allow the fish some running room. Let it go. Tighten your drag a little maybe to slow him. Although I never do this until I'm sure the fish is played out a little. I've lost too many tightening the drag before the fish is tired-he simply makes a hard, fast run and breaks me off, so I wait and play the fish. Give and take-tug of war. Give him some line, take back some line.

Do this until you feel the fish stop. He's done. Then reel him in. If he makes one last run, don't worry—it's more from desperation, he's tiring out. You're ready to land your dream.

First, however, to make that dream come true, the fisherman must learn to tie a strong knot, so there is one other consideration when choosing what line to use: braided line connects to knots much tighter and does not stretch as much when a big fish is pulling against it. It's flexible enough so that when the unexpected does come, your knot will not extend beyond the breaking point and snap like ordinary line, and your dream become lost.

I see this as a metaphor; stretch your relationships beyond the breaking point, man or woman, husband or wife, even business partner; if the relationship is built on a strong foundation, a tight well formed knot, when the pull comes as inevitably it must, if you are stretched too thin, though your knot may hold and you remain the best of friends, your line will snap and you will still lose everything.

You must develop a touch, something you can only learn by experience. A fisherman must fish all kinds of fish to correctly interpret the breaking point. The strongest knot may hold fast, but it does not matter if your line breaks.

What happened to my marriage, to many marriages, is this: the bond is strong, the knot tight; my wife and I were the best of friends and remain so to this day, but I was overextended, and the timing was not right. My line broke, and I lost everything.

We were each trying to do too many things at once (multi-tasking). I was not taking care of business at home. When I was pulled out to Los Angeles, to try to sell a screenplay, and a hurricane was threatening, and I did not come home--my wife walked out on me. I should've noticed the warning signs all around me, but I wanted that big fish too much. I went beyond the breaking point.

I did not have the discipline to wait, to work on the problems at hand, to play the fish and let it come to me. So I lost it.

The most important thing to remember about braided line is that so long as your knot holds, your line will not break.

There are four basic rules for the tying of knots, yet it's amazing how easy it is to go astray: The first, shaping, is the most important, get that wrong, even in the minutest detail, and the knot will slip or unravel at a critical moment.

If it is shaped correctly from the start, with all loops and lines in proper alignment, each wound in specific order then thread the end through, under, over and back through, when the time comes for it all to draw together, if applied with a steady, even pressure, it should tighten effortlessly.

Like any relationship, in which two people inevitably draw together, if the knot is not shaped right at the start, it will either become hopelessly entangled and fall apart, or it may have the appearance of exactitude but when tested will quickly unravel. Then you will have to start all over again.

The problem arises when the big fish are biting and you are tempted to go with what you have, with what you know is an inferior knot. Don't be fooled, when the moment of truth arrives, it will always fail you when you need it most. It's got to be tied right from the start.

If, in life for instance, you meet someone, and the relationship begins with a lie, or a falsehood, it may last for a time, but inevitably one day something will cause it to slip, and then to begin to unravel altogether. And you will be left with another broken hope or dream or ambition. Perhaps the man or woman of your dreams. Just because it was not tied true at the start. Better to start over and get it right from the beginning.

When a relationship begins in honesty and openness, with integrity and honesty, both parties stand a better chance of drawing together, like a well-formed knot, to form a true and lasting bond, which will hold when the pressure is on.

The first step in a relational knot is critical, for it leads on to the next. The drawing together, in which line to line, and loop to loop is methodically bonded to form a perfect union. For loop and line or man and woman, this is the most rewarding time.

You see your careful knot work pay off the first time it is tested, and you feel confident it will hold, come what may. The first test is always the worst—it is here where many a line and relationship breaks or simply unravels and we go our separate ways. But pass the first test, and it may lead on, to a lasting relationship, a happy marriage, success in business and a big fish on the docks.

It's almost sensuous the way it occurs. Wet your line with saliva to lubricate it; then as converging lines are drawn together, and the loops begin to tighten accordingly, everything will come together effortlessly as it should. It's a beautiful thing to see. The line tightening against the hook and holding strong. Everything working together.

Like two good people, they're made for each other and if tied correctly at the onset, nothing can pull them apart. Take care, however, many a fisherman has buried a hook in his hand as the knot was tightened down and slipped from his grasp. If it is not going to work, let it go. Save a lot of heartache.

As the knot moves, it should gently slide down the line to fasten itself. Never yank it or pull it too hard, or there will be a loose end. Go slow and be on your guard when everything looks too perfect. There might be a hook waiting somewhere.

It is now that you are ready to cut the ends off. All loose ends should be severed, keeping the knot trimmed close.

This keeps the hook and line clean and drag-free.

This principle may be applied to relationships with the application that the closer the bond, the more it should be kept free of any and all loose ends, previous relationships, past patterns of behavior, old baggage, anything that might tangle you or your partner. One snag is all it takes to lose a big fish or a big dream. Cut your loose ends short.

The first knot I learned to tie was the most difficult and the most demanding; it was also the most useful. Although technically called the Uni Knot, I call it the Snook Knot because, with it I caught my first <u>big</u> Snook, but I'm getting ahead of myself.

First I had to learn to tie the knot, to take it though its paces step by step. It was a long and arduous process.

At first my fingers fumbled with the intricate loops, which had to be drawn parallel, then doubled back upon itself with enough line to spare, as I held the line in the palm of one hand, while with my other hand I attempted to wind the end over itself five to seven times, over the main line, thread it through the smaller loop, then back through the larger loop, using my thumb as an anchor, which always seemed to get in my way. When I attempted to pull it tight, something always went awry. It was almost comical, pathological, as in pathos- sorrow, pity, as I tried, without success, over and over and over again, knowing in my heart, that if I didn't get this right – it was all over.

No matter how many times I tried I could not get it right. Something always went wrong. Like previous relationships and marriage, it never drew together correctly, and I had to start over. Or I would forget the sequence and the knot would tie, but it would tie too far up the line or only half-way and I'd have to cut it. The fit was wrong.

Then one day I got it. The problem was one of miscommunication: I was zigging when I should've been zagging. I was not listening to what the knot wanted.

A living object, it seemed to come to life in my hand never wanting to do what I wanted it to do, to go where I wanted it to go. It would twist when I wanted it to turn, like one of those wooden toys you had as a child, the snake that you hold near its tail as its head twists and turns, helter skelter.

The Uni was turning out to be a recalcitrant knot, stubborn and willful, the line with a life of its own. The harder I struggled to make it go the way I thought it should, the more it resisted. In the end it was a fine mess. Uni, from the prefix unity, meaning to come together as one, was definitely not working as its name implied.

How many relationships end this way? Because we refuse to allow our significant other room to grow, to become who they were meant to be, to shape their ends with us in a way that fits them, not us, and so we never completely come together as one. Each remains separate, in his or her own world, wondering what went wrong?

Furthermore, it becomes an absolute necessity to learn to tie a knot quickly by rote. In real-life conditions, inclement weather, when the wind is blowing, or big fish are biting hard and fast, and you are flying blind, it becomes necessary to be able to tie by memory, or you'll miss your chance, and watch it slip away before your eyes.

People are a lot like knots. Stubborn, demanding, wanting to go their own way, moving unpredictably aslant, throwing everything off. You have to know how to deal with the issues, in the thick of it, as they arise. You have to know how to smooth things out to proceed without a hitch.

Add to that a thousand other complications inherent in a day of fishing, or any relationship, and just when things are going well, and success is within your grasp, you are shocked to discover you have lost again. Why?

I repeat. It all begins and ends with the knot. Learn to tie it correctly or lose it all.

I persisted. I refused to quit, although many times I wanted to. It was boring, tying and retying the same knot over and over again. I thought I'd never get it.

Then I learned to let go, to let the line move without restraint in my hand, the way it was designed to. I learned to work with the line, allowing it the freedom to move on its own, the sinuous coils coming to life in my hand in one continuous motion. As soon as I did it became effortless. It came to me.

It took me about 20- 30 tries before I began to understand the true nature of a knot. Be it a love knot or a fishing knot. Only when you stop forcing it, do the lines to began to fall spontaneously into place, as if they know, with unerring instinct, borne and bred in the DNA of fishing line -- and of the human heart, the proper way to form a true and lasting knot.

Fish On!

As soon as I let it be itself, and stopped trying to impose my will on it, as if by magic, it allowed my hand to bend and shape it any way I wanted to. Now I can do it in my sleep. I use it all the time, in fishing and in life. In my relationships with my children I continually re-tie the knot, knowing as I do they need to be told I love them everyday. I forge the ties that bind every time I do. I know the knot will hold because I am a tier of good, strong and lasting knots.

With a woman I was dating, I showed her I respected her enough to trust her to know what was best for her. I stopped trying to tell her what to do, to control her life, and lo and behold—in time she came to me. It was wonderful, the knot sliding down, formed to fit this time, the disparate ends, line upon line, joining together in equality, two becoming one, individuals yet of a single strand. And so it goes.

I took great pride the day I finally got it right. At last the knot was tied correctly, and rode high above the leader and the hook, awaiting my touch to cinch it tight.

I was careful not to yank on it, for that would have been a violation of its spirit and from trail and error, it often ended in the knot popping loose before it hit the eye of the hook. Knots are not made to stand that sort of abuse, and neither are people. They require a more subtle touch.

Until you pull a knot tight, it is coiled and ready yet useless and slack; it requires the right touch to spring to life, for once it is pulled tight, it slides down against the hook and locks down securely, so the harder the fish pulls, the tighter it holds. That's the beauty of the Uni Knot. One line, looped around itself, joined together to form two, to strengthen and form one again at the point of contact.

Like any successful relationship, tighten the knot and you behold the urge to come together like lovers, entangled in each other's arms, loose the knot and you fall away breathless, one again, yet the ties that bind are stronger now than before, because, two, who were separate, unique and individual, have become one. And much stronger than they were alone. A relationship cannot survive without a knot. A lover's knot.

When I take the training wheels off my daughter's bike for the first time and she did not want to ride alone, because she fell and was afraid, I was there by her side. "You can do this," I whisper in her ear, "because you are strong. You may fall, but you will get up again."

She looks up at me. "Really?" she says, wiping a tear from her bright blue eyes.

"Yes," I answer and I feel the knot slip tight. It is a love knot and it will hold. It will hold.

And away she flies on her little pink and purple bike, streamers streaming out behind her, knees askance, holding on tight, ready to soar.

When my son asks me to fly paper airplanes on the beach, I honor him by spending time by his side folding the planes with him, when I would much rather be doing something else, something I consider more important. It is important to him, and I am there. From the beginning he has liked to use his hands. He's an artist. He likes to draw. To construct, build, fashion, to create. When he draws an amazing picture of sea-turtles swimming out to sea, which we discovered one morning on the beach and released, I frame it and put it on the wall of my house. And I feel the knot slip tight.

At sunset, we fly our paper airplanes on the beach, and I watch as his far out-sails mine, coming to a landing in the distance on the shore.

"You're amazing," I tell him. "So creative with your hands. One day you'll do great things."

He smiles, and I feel the knot slip tight. It too will hold. Forever.

16 Losing Heart: The Death of Dogs

The little brown body that lies in the garden, under the makeshift cross, bears the name, Heart. She was a dappled dachshund—a startlingly arresting, uniquely beautiful dog—with one wolfish blue eye and another, almost human brown one. Her coat was jet black, silver-blue and warm chocolate mixed, almost the color of hot coca, stirred in a mug, upon coming in from a cold winter's day.

She loved to go fishing with me, and would lope up and down the shores of Pass-a-Grille till I caught a Snook, then bark like mad and wag her tail as I reeled it in right under her nose. On numerous occasions, she accompanied me to Fort Desoto. The flats were never half as lonely when she was there. She was a fishing dog.

She was all heart. With the sweet poetry of her being, she would literally turn herself inside out and upside down every time I walked through the door.

She was my best friend.

She died in my arms last night.

I remember the day we got her. She was so small she fit into the palm of our hands. We drove all the way to North Tampa to get her.

My daughter, Phoebe, fell asleep in the back seat. When we arrived, Heart's owner handed me the little pup through the window. Gently, I set the dog in my daughter's lap and drove away.

Halfway across the Howard Franklin Bridge, I gazed into my rearview mirror. Phoebe was smiling from ear to ear.

"What shall we name it," I inquired.

Phoebe bit her lip, staring off into space and thought for a long moment. "Heart!" She said, "because she's my heart."

We drove to the Sunflower School to pick up my son, Sky. Just as class was getting out, I held Heart up through the sunroof. His face lit up and he ran to us under the towering oak tree, scooped the pup into his arms and pressed his cheek against it.

Driving home, I once again glanced into the rearview. Their gracious little heads were nearly touching, in a timeless, never to be forgotten moment of childhood innocence as they gazed tenderly at their new puppy, running their hands through her soft, silky fur.

Heart's best buddy was our tiger-striped tabby cat, Milkfoot. They would tussle by the hour, Heart's fangs at the cat's throat, the cat's claws buried in the dog's fur, yet never once did they harm each other. The true claws and fangs remained sheathed as they romped and played.

We enjoyed the pleasure of Heart's company for almost two years. She died a few weeks short of her second birthday, which we had been looking forward to, so we could throw her a party and present her with some new toys. She always liked getting toys. Toys with which she will never play.

The death of dogs in a serious matter, more like losing a beloved family member than a pet. This was not a glamorous Hollywood death, or a death from afar, as in hearing about it and saying how sorry you are, this was death up close, down on my knees, sobbing, weeping, praying, while I watched her suffer her death agonies, trying to hold her head up, gasping for breath, as she drowned in the elixir of her own asphyxiation.

It took her all night to die. It was not a pretty sight, but I did not turn away.

I was there with her to the last breath. I sang her a little lullaby, which I used to sing to my children whey they were quite young. I rocked her gently in my arms, easing her way.

She would become still for awhile, breathe deeply, even serenely, then the trembling would begin again. The look of pain was in her eyes and with it, the involuntary neurological convulsions, which rocked her, slowly shutting down her vital organs. She finally died at 4:55 in the morning. In my arms, in bed beside me, at peace.

Once, during the prolonged death watch I assured her, "I'm here, girl, it's OK." She half-heartedly tried to wag her tail. That for me, was the saddest moment. That and a series of long, plaintive wails, as if she were begging for her life, and did not want to go.

The Vet had taken her off her medicine, so she was aware of my presence. It was in her eyes.

The tragic thing is, she died twice, like a shipwreck survivor, that swims through dangerous waters all night only to drown within sight of shore.

She had swallowed a small rubber capsule of some sort off the beach, which then became lodged in her intestines. With the stoicism of animals, she had crawled up under the house to die. I did not know where she was for a day and a half. Fortunately, we discovered her in time and took her to the vet.

The emergency operation was a success. Dr. Frank Mills, a good man with a dog, saved her life. He was in surgery for three hours. Heart spent the night there recuperating, replenishing her electrolytes.

The day after her surgery, when we returned, Heart was her old self, sitting up, barking and wagging her tail. Happy to see us.

The children were ecstatic. They reached through the bars of the cage, soothing her with cries of love and devotion. Heart had stitches in her abdomen and had to wear a cone on her head to keep from biting or scratching them free.

We laughed and joked about changing her name to Cone-head. We took her home and went out for a little walk. She seemed fine, on the mend, through a little awkward as she tried to maneuver with the cone.

That night, I awoke to find her standing in the bathroom, wavering slightly from side to side and staring at the wall. She was lost. The following morning, when I took her out for a walk, she fell over onto her side.

"Come on, girl," I coaxed, but she could not get up. We took her back to the doctor's office and left her there for observation for the night. She was alive the next morning, but no better. The prognosis was not good, yet we still had hope. Something had gone off in her head like a neurological time bomb. There was nothing more the doctor could do, so he recommended a neurological specialist in Sarasota. It was Friday, the specialist was away until Monday, so we took Heart home for a little TLC.

She was so blue. The cone bothered her.

At first I thought she was going to make it, but later as her condition worsened, and she could not stop shaking, I was not sure. Already traumatized from spending so much time away from home, being poked and prodded, stitched and cut, I took the cone off her head and let her lie still awhile. She put her head between her paws and gazed at me forlornly. I could tell it was her way of saying goodbye.

About an hour before her imminent death, she began to run in place, lying flat on her side, her tongue hanging out, until finally she closed her eyes and lay still, then breathed her last.

I felt her go—out through my fingertips.

At her funeral we paid our last respects by recalling a precious memory of her and leaving a little memento, a keepsake of our love and affection, by her graveside. I buried her body between two flowering Hibiscus trees in the garden and covered her with a paving stone, upon which she used to lie in the sun.

"What do you remember?" I asked my daughter, Phoebe.

"Her little wet nose," was her reply. "And the way she used to sit on the table and watch me do my ABC'S." Phoebe lay a little red and white bobber down by her side. "Because she was a fishing dog," she said.

My son, Sky spoke movingly of the way Heart used to curl up beside him at night. I think he missed her the most, because Heart had bonded to him most strongly.

As we bowed our head in prayer a shaft of sunlight rent the clouds and shone down onto the paving stone, between the two Hibiscus. Her grave was lit by a light from above. Highly unusual, we all noted it.

Later that night, around nine o'clock, the cat was restless, so I let her out. About midnight, I went looking for her. She was curled on the paving stone, her head on her paws, asleep. At her feet lay a dead lizard, an offering to her dear departed friend.

Death changes you. Makes you value life more dearly than before. It forces you to pause in your relentless pursuit, to just stop.

I felt like a clock that had wound down, the hands frozen in time. To re-wind myself and carry on, I had to take a gut check.

In English the word Heart is a derivative of courage, from the prefix "cour," in French. It means living with a quality of inner strength, to face anything that is difficult or painful, without drawing away.

Lose heart, lose everything. Take heart, my friends, take heart. Honor the people in your lives with courage in their hearts; the ones who stand with you when the chips are down. The ones with heart. That is why I respect and admire fishermen and women. They face the elemental everyday, the sun and the wind, storms and changing tides and seasons with courage and conviction, for death, if anything, is about courage, the courage to go on living, to find meaning in life, to go on--even when it seems that all is lost. One moment your loved one is there, warm and breathing, the next-, like a puff of smoke on the wind, they're gone. Accessible only in memory now.

When all your dreams die hard- courage! When you feel you can't go on-courage! When it seems there is no hope—courage!

There are no easy answers, but I take away three essential insights into the nature of death: death, even among the least of us, diminishes every one. Something in us dies too. Second: However it comes, in whatever form, at the moment of actual death, endorphins—natural pain-killers in the brain—kick in, and our actual physical demise may not be so difficult, you simply slip away at the end in one last breath—then peace. Lastly, although you suffer loss, it is also a blessing. I have been present at two deaths and two births, and basically they are the same. After much pain and suffering, we awaken somewhere else, into another world, in death—a better one.

The following night I dreamt of Heart. She was running in green fields beside a river filled with golden Snook, together with a man whose back was turned away from me.

As they walked along, side by side, the man reached down and patted Heart. His hands were large and rough, like that of a fisherman or a carpenter. Perhaps they were going fishing.

Mysterium Tremendum!

It was God Himself, Creator of heaven and earth—of all things great and small—even dogs. And as I watched, He scooped Heart up into his arms and held her close into His loving heart, into the ground of all being—the big, warm beating heart of God's own love, of love itself.

I realized, although her body lies beneath the paving stone in the garden, beneath the wooden cross, her spirit is with the One who made her, who loves her, who walks with her through green fields—her true Master. I like to think that it was He to whom she was running in her final hour. Into His loving arms.

Ever since the first wild wolf, Canis Familaras, reached across the natural divide to sleep beside the fire at the hearths of man, the dog has been our best friend. And what is dog spelled backwards but the great *I AM!*

17 Lesson Of The Strike Zone

In any body of water in Florida, there is a school of fish swimming just below the surface. The lesson is to learn about water. But there is a lot of water and water columns to cover, and to use a baseball analogy, the strike zone (about three feet) may be as small as the one at home plate. Find it, and you will hit a home run, miss and you strike out. To further the analogy, it's the best way to acquire an Inshore Slam, the Grand Slam of fishing, that is locating three different species, a trout, a red-fish and a Snook, all on the same day, and catching all three, each in its own strike zone. Fun!

It takes practice, but once you learn how to find it—you will catch fish after fish after fish, while all around you, others catch nothing. It may seem like magic, but there is tried and tested logic behind it.

Always bring at least two or three separate rods and reels, rigged for different situations: I bring one rigged for live bait; one for lures, and one Sabiki, for live bait: pin-fish or greenbacks. I usually have a bucket of live shrimp on hand as well, just in case.

To find the strike zone I first cast a lure and play it through the water, up-current, down-current, straight out—If nothing hits, I try a live shrimp, free-lined. If I don't get a bite on that I use a sabiki to catch a pinfish or greenie; I hook the greenback just above the pectoral fin, which will make it swim down into the strike zone at the lower water columns, where the big fish are, and see if I get a hit. If I don't get a strike, I nose-hook a pin-fish, and let it swim with the shallower current so it lays true in the tide.

In this way I analyze the different levels of the water column and strike zones: up-current, down-current and straight out in front of me, deep, medium depth and shallow with a variety of baits and approaches. If you are targeting deep water fish, always use a heavier leader and a larger egg-type sinker; if your target is fish that swim in the middle of the water column, use a lighter weight-both leader and sinker. If you are targeting the top of the water column, use top-water plugs and lures with light leader and no weight. Learn to cast accurately from a distance, so that you can hit the strike zone without added weight.

If you do this—you will get hit. Nine times out of ten. When it happens I take note and repeat the process, aiming for precisely the same location, using the same bait.

Casting is crucial. Set up a target. Practice the art of casting until you can hit the bulls-eye. Because that's where the fish will be.

There's a school of fish out there somewhere, count on it-- so try, try again—find the strike zone, and you will get hit. Again and again and again. While ten yards away a fisherman sits idly and watches as you pull in one after another and wonders why? Now you know one of the best kept secrets of all. Swing for the grandstands.

The second knot I mastered, the Blood Knot, made it easier for me to find the strike zone. It fulfilled the need to join two different fishing lines, of different weights and consistencies, together, line to line. If I wanted to free-line a shrimp or pinfish up under the mangroves and let it drift back down to dangle in front of a Snook's mouth, I had to make it look as light and as natural as possible, yet keep the line strong because Snook will run back into the mangroves and snap or snag the line on the roots.

If I wanted to join braided line to fluorocarbon straight to a lure, without the interference of a leader or a swivel, I had to learn to tie two different lines together in a tight, unbreakable knot, then use another knot, the loop knot to tie on the lure.

With a long leader only one knot is required to join line to leader, but if you have not learned to tie that one yet, a small swivel at one end may suffice to join the braided line to your leader; tie the swivel tight, however, with a good strong knot because a swivel is just another weak link.

With braided line, such as Power Pro, don't use a clinch knot to tie the swivel to your braid, because it will tend to slip on Power Pro's slick surface. Ordinarily a swivel is a good thing, allowing the bait to spin and swirl in the currents, but the Apex predators have incredible eyesight and a latch or a swivel may give away your presence, and using these with a lure is futile, so tying a line to line is the best, most versatile knot I know, but it is difficult to learn and requires patience and practice.

With snaps, and latches and swivels, too much pressure from a big fish and the latch may spring and pull the hook loose right from the fish's mouth.

Big Snook will often perform this trick. You pull your line up, and the latch will be bent out of shape, and your hook-- missing, so a latch is not the best hardware for big fish. It slips. And little slips can lead to big losses. Especially when it counts.

Ultimately it's best to tie braid to a 36-50 inch long fluorocarbon leader, because Snook have such acuity of vision that it is difficult for a fisherman to use a lot of hardware, and catch this elusive prey on a consistent basis. You may get lucky and do it-once. Not twice.

Because most fisherman use monofilament leaders, Snook see it, and avoid it. They will easily spook and pass you by, all things being equal, if they spot anything out of the ordinary.

The use of fluorocarbon for Snook is more effective. Tying sturdy braided line to a simple fluorocarbon leader in a blood-knot, then tying a Uni straight to the hook is a sure way to catch more fish —especially Snook.

Eventually I bought my own spools of fluorocarbon, and measured off my own leaders, each about 36-44 inches, then tied it straight to the braid in a blood knot.

I then tied the fluoro leader directly to a light wire circle hook, with as little interference between the line, the hook and the fish as possible. Then I simply hooked live bait on the hook, a large select shrimp, a pin-fish or a greenie, and cast out, free-lining.

Sometimes, when the current was swift, I use a small split-shot to keep the bait down in the water column where the big fish swim.

Once I learned how to tie a good strong, secure knot, with braid, and to play it right, I never lost a fish again. In the summer of 2005, during the Red Tide, believe it or not, I caught over 100 large Snook, and lost not one.

The first Snook I ever hooked and landed, came because I finally understood the concept of the strike zone. And I caught it on a pin-fish.

Ha!

The sky was overcast, of a late afternoon in June. I was walking by the Snook Wall and I saw a school of Snook, the water roiling around the female. They were mating. I watched in fascination for about ten minutes. Then the school broke up.

I cast in approximately where I last saw the school. The moment the bait hit the water, my pole bent double and line started screaming out. The drag sang my name.

They were hungry you see, after mating. If ever you see a Snook mating ball, although you may be tempted, do not cast out into the middle of it right away. You will only break it up and they will swim away. Wait.

When you see the school break up, then cast out nearby. You will have a school of famished fish in the water. Soon there will be a feeding frenzy of hungry Snook.

When I hooked my first big Snook, I knew why I had hooked it. It was not luck this time-I expected it. As I tried to lift my rod tip, I cursed, for I thought I'd lost the fish and was snagged; it was so heavy, almost like I had the bottom-- then the line started moving again—out into the deeper water.

It couldn't be that big. No way!

Way!

I reeled in, trying to remain calm, to remember to breathe. It turned toward the shore and I ran down the wall with it, drag singing, line playing out.

In my heart I knew what I had on the line.

As I fought it in, a large accumulation of bubbles rose steadily from the bottom to the surface, like a diver was down there, or the Creature of the Black Lagoon. Then slowly up it rose in a flash of gold. A fish half as large as I was. A Snook!

I had finally caught and landed a Snook.

I leapt off the wall and ran into the water, afraid it was going to get away, but it did not. I had hooked it securely in the jaw, and, wonder of wonders, the knot had held. I unhooked it and held it up to my eyes. I wished this feeling would last forever. It was wonderful!

In my excitement I let it go—I loved it. It swam away with the current. I danced back down the beach.

On the Snook wall where I fished, between 2nd and 3rd Avenue on the east side of Pass-A-Grille, there were three other fishermen that day.

"Hey," they wanted to know, "how do you do that?" I laugh inwardly, remembering the Snook Whisperer.

Might as well try to explain how Leonardo painted the Mona Lisa's smile, capturing the essence of a woman's mystery on canvas; how Shakespeare composed his lyrical Sonnets, with their eternal rhyme; how Stradavari constructed his violins, from an ordinary block of wood, the same dull timber used by other Luthiers, yet his strings sing beneath the bow unlike any other.

I turn and walk the other way, trying to escape. As I do I whisper the Snook's secret name to see if it works. I had forgotten till now. Low and behold I get another hookup, and reel it in, playing it like a Stradivarius right under the other fisherman's noses.

"He's using live bait!" Cries one, the one with the beer gut and the childishly over long shorts, reaching half-way down his legs.

"He's free-lining," shouts another, wearing his ball-cap on backwards.

They follow me in single file down the wall.

I cast out into the deeper, darker bluer water and reel in a little to let the current carry it back into the shallower, aqua-green water, nearer the shore—right into the strike zone.

I know exactly where this lies because I live here and I have studied the underwater terrain, which now lies hidden from view. But at low tide, when the water is clear, a natural shelf emerges hidden just beneath the rocks.

I put on a mask and snorkel and enter the fishes' realm.

There I have seen Snook, by the hundreds, stacked up in their secret spot, waiting for a live bait to swim into their purview. I have observed their behavior, from a fishes' eye view, so to speak, and now I understand them better. As a predator they lay in wait.

A fisherman must time it perfectly, however, so that the live bait swims naturally from out of the deeper water into the shallower, dropping at an accurate incline beneath the shelf, and falls, not directly in front of the Snook's nose, and spooks it, nor too near their tails and they miss it, but just ever so, somewhere between infinity and eternity: Leonardo, it is said, haunted the gallows, following the gravediggers to the cemetery, to perform experiments on cadavers, dissecting the muscle from the bone, so that when he brushed the paint onto his canvas, to more closely approximate the plasticity of flesh, the faces of his portraits would pulsate with anatomically correct life; Shakespeare's folios, historians note, are printed from the original without flaw, error or grammatical correction, as if the inspired words were dictated to the poet from on high; thousands of violins were handcrafted during the Golden Age, yet only one—The Stradivarius still rings with the spirit of its creator—Stadavari, who with his finely tuned wood-worker's ear, created a living, breathing instrument, whose quality, pitch and tone remain unequaled to this day.

Snook Whisperers all.

"Look!" He's talking to the water," says one of the fisherman, the one with a tattoo stenciled across his back:"BORN TO LOSE."

They have seen but not heard me whisper the secret name. And I hook another big Snook. I set the drag and listen to it sing its sweet song. I reel in another fish right under their noses. Another big Snook. For I have found the strike zone.

This annoys and exasperates them. Their hooks fly by my ear wantonly. They're using these big, expensive rigs, sinkers, bobbers, swivels, snaps. Trying a little bit of everything I guess.

I duck just in time and pull up my fish. I am so happy I do a little jig right there on the wall.

"Look. He's doing a Snook dance," cries Tattoo.

Immediately all three begin to imitate my little dance, hoping somehow it will help them. They watch my next cast and time theirs perfectly to mine, casting in all at once, managing to foul our lines, so that now everyone's lines are entangled in a big, twisted mess.

"Thanks, guys."

Incredibly, out of all the crossed lines, their sinkers pulling me down, their bobbers, yanking my line this way and that on the current, I hook another Snook and reel it in right under their incredulous noses.

To a man, they catch nothing.

They all crack open their tackle-boxes and attempt to emulate my direct line to leader approach. Only, when it comes down to it, they don't know how. Too busy pretending.

If they had asked, I could have told them: fish on-- during the hottest, dog days of summer, in the sweltering heat and humidity of July and August in Florida, the threat of heat-stroke a constant reality, as the sweat pours into your eyes and blinds you while you attempt to thread yet another complex knot, broken off, or tangled through wind-lash, the angry rumble of thunder booming in your ears, as yet another hurricane hurtles your way, the lightning flashing across a low, claustrophobic sky as dark as doomsday; while you stand and cast out among choking weeds, the stench of Red Tide in your nostrils, the scarcity of live bait, forcing you to either improvise and net your own bait on the spot, free-lining on the move, or master the use of a lure.

And still you slog on day in, day out, when everyone else has long since quit and gone home, developing a deft and subtle touch for that elusive Snook, so that you know how to set the hook when the time comes.

They were using dead shrimp and large egg sinkers. Might as well remove the hook. I would have told them to throw it all away—to forget what they thought they knew about fishing. Simplify. Get rid of all adornments, bobbers, sinkers, latches, swivels if you want to catch fish. Line to line to hook. And fish the strike zone in the water columns.

Keep it simple. All they had to do was look at my rig when I pulled up yet another Snook. It was right in front of their eyes. But they wouldn't have seen it anyway. Too busy trying to impress each other. Funny how the simplest things remain the most illusive to understand, the most difficult to comprehend.

Our ego gets in the way; we all want to look like we know what we are doing, so we tie all kinds of hardware onto bigger and better poles. The more the better, we think.

My simple, unpretentious rig, must've looked like a magic wand to them. Abra Cadabra! Fish on.

So many people running around trying everything they can think of, using everything they can find, trying to make a good impression, when in truth, the simple things are best.

The biggest rod and reel, the bigger house, the faster car or boat, the trophy wife or girlfriend, the biggest and the best of everything. On the surface.

Yet deep down these things will not satisfy us nor will they help to catch the big dream because they are only an illusion-an image. Most fishermen I know see beyond that- into the strike zone.

They have humbled themselves to learn from others, for there are many masters in fishing, and each has some knowledge to impart. Yet gruff and unpretentious, the fishing masters do not suffer fools gladly. You must accept this gift humbly, on one knee.

What I have may not look like much, but what I have is real. I let it all go. That's fishing at its best—and life, the way it should be lived. Keep only what works. Ditch the rest. Then go looking for the strike zone.

Line to line with nothing coming in between, tied off with a good strong knot. It may seem invisible, but there is a strategy at work. A strategy strong enough to hold a big love, a big fish or an even larger dream. Make sure there is nothing that comes between you and your heart's desire. Line to line, heart to heart.

18 Land's End: Lesson Of The Cobia

Medieval knights, in their search for the grail, had in their retinue, a young protégé, or squire to aid and assist them on their quest. Fishing, as a quest of sorts, is what the Knights referred to as a "long desire," the longing for something unattainable, just out of reach." I, as a Knight of the Kingdom by the Sea of Pass-A-Grille, have three squires: Dave, Shane and Johnnie, ages, 16, 17 and 13.

Of the three, Dave, a cherubic teen with a baby face, is by far the best and most passionate fisherman, although Shane will give him a run for his money on any given day, at any given time. Through every kind of weather, in calm and in storm, night or day, Dave fished on as if driven on by some unseen force. He fished anywhere, anytime: the Skyway, Redington Long Pier, the Downtown pier, the flats at Fort Desoto, yet in his heart his favorite fishing spot will always be here on Pass-A-Grille.

With instructions to call my cell-phone in the event of a fishing opportunity, he seemed to ring every time I sat down to write, his voice excited, exuberant—breathless. His joy, irresistible and contagious, never failed to whisk me back to the days of my own youth, when fishing was everything. With my father in the Caribbean, or on the sun-baked docks at Cedar Key, along the muddy banks of Hogtown, or wading knee deep in the flats of Watermelon Pond, the stately oaks hung with long gray beards of Spanish Moss, a Snowy White Egret, silhouetted against the eternal, cloudless blue skies of childhood.

"You've got to come out to the jetty!" He'd wail. "There's a school of AJ's, and I've got pinfish, dude."

"I can't right now," I'd rant, trying to sound busy, then on second thought—"are they big jacks?"

"Yeah! Boiling right in front of me. Forty or fifty." Then I'd hear him shout-"Fish on!" And away I'd go, fishing rod in hand. Dave was my eyes and ears on Pass-A-Grille. He knew where to find the action, day or night. Sometimes, just as I was settling in at night, half-asleep, the phone would ring and there was that voice again. "Dude! There's Snook everywhere! Shane and I are on the wall. You coming?"

In the background I'd hear a frenzied shout—"fish on!" And that was it—nothing could keep me away. I'd run down the block to the east, and there they stood like an angler's dream, balanced along the edge of the what was to become known as the Snook Wall, lines out into the water, whooping and hollering with delight. They greeted me like a long-lost brother, the largest Spanish Sardine in the bait bucket, always reserved for me. They would offer it up with a kind of reverence, bestowing on me the best they had to offer. I'd mount the wall, in a single bound and fall into place beside them, casting out into the darkness, in a race to be the first to cry—"Fish on!"

Later, we'd move it out to the jetty to go shark fishing at mid-night, the currents ripping wildly past us in the moonlight, the possibilities endless. Sometimes I'd awake my son and daughter and they would join us for a night of fishing beneath the full moon. Shane always made my daughter, Phoebe laugh out loud with his lame jokes, while Dave tutored my son in the fine points of fishing for shark from a jetty at night.

It was all quite a thrill, and each time I saw Dave and Shane walking around the streets of Pass-A-Grille, my heart skipped a beat, for I knew that soon I would be joining in the fun, fishing with kindred spirits who loved the sport as much as I.

Though they were teenagers, somehow they had managed to escape the ravages of our pop culture; they were beyond it, or so I thought. These were happy, wholesome, remarkably self-reliant adolescents. So many of our children are content to lay around the house and watch TV or pretend, that with the repetitious push of a button on a mind-numbing video game, they have mastered something real, a virtuosity of the void.

Not so these boys: Dave and Shane have ventured out into the real world, with its difficulties and dangers and mastered something authentic, on a quest for something beyond their reach—a long desire. They have learned to tie their own knots, catch their own bait, spool their own line, and sharpen their own hooks. They interact with people from every walk of life, for the fishing community is a virtual United Nations of world-wide international citizenry. These fortunate few have felt the wind on their faces, the sun at their backs, and with discipline and character, set forth to challenge the sea, to win or lose in the game of life on their terms—a real game with high stakes.

Yet adolescence is a time of testing; no one escapes unscathed.

The last time I fished with Dave, a younger boy, Johnnie, or John as he prefers to be called, was hanging out along the Snook Wall. To John fell the duty of carrying an assortment of gear: rods and reels, bait buckets, heavy tackle.

He struggled beneath the burden, but Dave and Shane were, in their way, teaching him to be a fisherman, so he accepted his role, humbling himself under the often cruel and callous taunts of the older boys.

We stood on the wall fishing a high, outgoing tide, when I saw a large stingray swimming by on top of the water column.

I cast out, hoping for a bit of fun, when out from under the outstretched wingtips of the great ray, like a brown stealth bomber, shot a big Cobia, and inhaled my pinfish on the run. Hit and run, slash and burn-that is the Cobia for you. Always be on the lookout for stingrays. Cobia often travel in pairs under their wings.

The Cobia hit and hit hard. So hard in fact, that it wrenched me off the wall, and dragged me down the beach. I had to run to keep up with it. The line was un-spooling fast—too fast. As ever, Dave was at my side. He leapt down and raced along the beach ahead of me, alerting the other fishermen who lined the shore.

"Fish on! Fish on!" He shouted, arms flailing. I ducked beneath the line of fisherman and pumped hard to check the fish, and win back some line, but discovered to my dismay, the line was still running out. Apparently, there was no stopping this fish in its blistering run. So I let it go and set my ear to the pitch of the drag as it sang.

I tightened the drag slightly to slow it or at least tire it, locked in a tug of war with something irreconcilably powerful at the other end, neither of us giving an inch. When I looked up, on the run, the dock at Land's End was rapidly approaching. The fish swam out, way past the dock and the line, slanted against the piling, yanked taught like a violin string tuned to the highest pitch and ready to snap.

Assessing the situation I thought there was no way I could do this. I was going to have to maneuver around the pilings of the dock if I had a prayer to land this monster. To do that I was going to have to wade out around the end- the dock juts some twenty to twenty five yards out into the sea, and the outgoing tide was raging over my head and the current, fast and furious.

I made my decision. "My sandals," I shouted. "Take them off, I'm going in."

John bent down and unlatched my sandals and set them in the sand. I rushed into the surging waves, which rushed through the pilings holding up the dock.

The water level rose to my shoulders, the current threatening to knock me off my feet and sweep me, my rod and reel away.

"I can't hold him," I shouted, hoisting the rod and reel above my head to keep it from getting drenched, while with the other, I clung to a piling, in an effort to avoid being swept off my feet.

Sizing up the situation, John climbed up onto the dock, raced to the end where I stood pinned chest deep beneath the pilings, in rushing water, line still spinning out from my reel. The strain was incredible. I could not hold on much longer. Either I would have to let go of the piling or the rod and reel.

"Up here, quick." It was John bent over the dock, his fingertips straining to reach the pole. There was nothing else to do, but accept his help; I could not have done it alone.. I lifted my rod and reel up to him, and he took over, enjoying himself immensely. Though guilty of trespassing, he fished on at the end of the dock at Land's End.

"Johnnie!" I snapped, using the baby name I knew he loathed. I had fought my way through the pilings, straining to walk amid the raging current. Yet it made me happy to see the boy enjoying himself, and I was thankful for his impulsive yet intuitive act, which had saved the day.

The fish was still on.

Dave, already on the far side, was waiting for me. "I got your back," he said.

"Hand it down," he commanded up to John, and good squire that he is, John complied. Dave held the pole tight without wavering till I reached the other side and we exchanged it on the run, like a relay racer, without so much as a pause in the action.

Incredibly—the line was still running out. 250 yards of braid, spooled off. I was down to the mono backing. Yards left before the fish broke me off.

This fish is going to pull me all the way to the jetty, I thought. With this tide, if he took me out that deep, I would have to cut the line and let him go, or go under myself and swim all the way to Mexico with the fish.

"Turn him into the current, tire him out." It was Dave. Good advice, remember that if you ever find yourself surf fishing and hooked to a big, blistering fish that you cannot stop. Turn him into the current, so he has to work.

I walked down the shoreline ahead of the fish and reeled it in backwards, making him swim against the current. It worked. The fish tired and stopped, with maybe a yard left on the spool. I reeled in the heavy load; it was coming closer now, I could see it in the clear green water rushing past my knees: long and stream-lined. A Brown Bomber with a stripe. It had been 20-30 minutes since I hooked the fish. My arms ached as the sweat poured into my eyes. My throat had gone dry, my tongue swollen.

"Water," I husked. I tried to swallow, but could not.

Dave unscrewed the top of an ice- cold bottled water and poured it over my head into my mouth. It was refreshing. "Go out and bring your fish in," he said. "Don't horse it."

I waded further out, waist-deep and reeled in my fish. It came easily, but there was still some fight left in it. A large Cobia, easily 40-50 pounds swam into view. When it reached my knees, I touched the leader as my slender 6'6 8-12 pound rod bent double—light tackle for a fish that big, and with a flick of its powerful tail, it ran with the current, doubling its speed and snapped my 30 pound braid like a thread.

"Damn!" I said, tired but happy. Though I had lost, it was the fight that mattered. I fought it from the seawall in the east, facing Boca Ciega Bay, around, under and over the dock at Land's End up to my shoulders in a surging sea, to the south along the crescent of shore, which sweeps south towards Eggmont Key in the distance, halfway toward the jetty in the west. 180 degrees almost. I sat down on the sand and took a deep breath, then another and another. It felt good to breathe again

"You brought it up to your knees, and touched the leader," Dave said. "That's good enough. We'll count it. You landed it."

"Thanks," I said. In that one word was everything.

When we got back to the wall, John's mother was waiting to pick him up.

"I hope he didn't get in your way too much."

"On the contrary," I replied. "I couldn't have done it without him."

A look of pride crossed his handsome young face. He was one of us now.

"I'll be back," he grinned as he climbed into the car.

"We'll get him next time," I smiled a little sadly.

Dave and I watched him go. "He was good today," Dave mused.

"So were you," I added. "You guys helped me in my quest for the big one."

"Is that what you want?" asked Dave.

"Yes, " I answered truly. "And what do you want?"

"To stay here and fish forever."

"Me too."

"But there won't be a next time for me. I won't be coming back," Dave confided.

"What!"

"My parents got a divorce. I'm going to Utah to spend the summer with my dad. When I get back we're moving to New Jersey. My mother's already bought a house."

I didn't know what to say. Dave had never really opened up before. Our relationship had revolved mainly around fishing, yet I had always sensed that something was driving him on. He fished too hard, too often, like his life depended on it. A magnificent obsession.

I remembered what the Snook Whisperer had said about me, and I thought I understood. I could only guess at the sense of loneliness he felt, the sense of abandonment, or given his attachment to Pass-A-Grille, a place not really his home, what his private life must've been like.

"They say there's big Striped Bass in Jersey," I added lamely.

The last time I saw him was a few nights later when he knocked on my door at half-past mid-night. He stood framed in my doorway, his face lost in the shadows.

"The Snook are biting," he said, though his voice had lost some of its luster. "Under the dock at Land's End."

I wish I could tell you I joined him for one last fishing quest together—one last long desire, but I was tired that night, so I stayed home. The next day I heard from Shane that they slayed them under the dock that night, and that Dave was gone.

The lesson of the Cobia is one of the most important of all: it takes guts—a leap of faith. Land's End: the point at which we can go no further together. From there we venture out on our own, into the world alone—beyond the safe, secure perimeter of land, past family, friends and home, into the unknown sea to brave the surging tides, which sweep us toward our destiny.

You must go beyond the point of no return. You must believe in yourself long after everyone has stopped believing in you.

The current is strong and swift-lose your footing and you may go under. It helps if you have a friend who's got your back. For if fishing is the quest, friendship is the Holy Grail.

19 Last Ticket To Paradise

There was the first faint presence of a fishing boat moving softly through the fog, heading out to sea at dawn—the moment crystallizing in my consciousness as my first iconic image of Pass-a-Grille. I was alone on the deserted strip of beach at Land's End.

There were no tall houses then, standing along the eastern shore. The fields were empty, a site for nesting terns. It was 1981.

Ten years later, I stood once again on the eastern seawall, which runs the length of Boca Ciega Bay and cast out my line, fishing for something, which I could only half-hope for; I saw a beautiful girl, down by the seashore, knee-deep in the water, with eyes the color of Paraiba Tourmaline; as she stooped to gather the folds of her long white sundress with one hand, her dark, windblown hair in the other, and the two images fused and froze into one—and a girl I'll never know became my second imprimatur of Pass-a-Grille.

The boat stood as a metaphor for something mystical, magical, the girl for romance and love. Only later did I come to realize that both were a part of something larger, but there was to be a third symbol, which has haunted me forever since, and which reminds me of what I have irretrievably lost and lost forever.

The bells of Pass-a-Grille. Evander's lovely bells. Happy, yet sad. Even now, they ring out loud and clear, riding the winds of change. Whenever I hear them, wherever I am, whatever I am doing—I pause, close my eyes and pretend I'm back again, back in that Pass-a-Grille that once was.

When I first heard the sad, sweet music of the bells, 27 years later, in 2006, I was standing on the same spit of shore at the southern tip of Pass-a-Grille, down around Land's End fishing-only this time everything had changed. The pure, clear ring of the clarion bells in the crisp, autumn air, swept me back in a sacrament, like a shrove-tide, back to a time when Pass—a-Grille was a sleepy little fishing village, when there were no bridges to the mainland, when the streets were paved with white sand; and even further back to the early Spanish explorers who caught their fish in the pass, and grilled them on the beach, not far from the very spot where I now stood, and from which Pass-a-Grille derives its name" The Pass of the Grillers.

The bells take me back. I see them now, their fires lighting up the sky. Singing, dancing, eating around the roaring fire, the fish laid out across the wood, the dripping fat, sizzling up in smoke from the open pits.

I go farther back in time- to the first fishermen who walked these shores-the original Indians, who hunted and fished this enchanted paradise, who drank water from three fresh-water wells, springs, bubbling up from the earth; Pass-a-Grille was the only barrier island with fresh water springs, cool, fresh drinking water.

An antique map of the state of Florida, drawn in 1776 by Bernard Romans, shows the Bay of Tampa, and specifically Pass-a-Grille, designated on the map with the words, "Espiritu Santo," which translated from the Spanish means "Holy Spirit." The Spanish interpreted the name from the Indians, their primary source, as the original people regarded Pass-a-Grille as holy ground.

There is an Indian legend, so long as the people of Pass-a-Grille remain pure of heart, nothing can harm this charmed spot of land.

The bells stop and I am back again. Today the many McMansions that crown the once pristine, deserted shore-line across the bay, blot out the sun as it rises in the east.

They stand shoulder to shoulder, to cast their looming shadow across the once empty land. Now cars are everywhere, and lines of people waiting to cross the street like Disneyworld. Tour busses whiz by, spewing diesel fumes into the air, tourists hanging out the windows, as someone bellows into a bullhorn. Even the sky is no longer sacred. Planes buzz low, towing banners across the sky advertising Tiki Bars, promoting wet-T shirt contests, the latest gin, vodka and rum drink for the crowds below. The tree-lined streets of Pass-a-Grille have become a vast, numbered parking lot. Every space is taken.

I walk over to the jetty, but a vast RV parks itself in front of the horizon, cutting off the view, as a family climbs out and races to the beach. When I get to the jetty, instead of the once deserted, melancholy promontory, there is a crowd of fishermen, elbow to elbow, each jostling for position, lines fouling, cursing, shouting—the Spanish Mackerel are running.. I turn and walk away. I prefer to fish in peace.

The trolley rolls past. All aboard. Last ticket to paradise.

Where then, does this leave the once quiet little community—Pass-a-Grille, literally at Land's End. This unspoiled isle, that flowered once, for untamed Indians' eyes. The humble fisherman's cottages, the colorful shanties, made from the wood of crab-traps, like the house in which I live—all carpentry finished in tongue and groove—not like the homes of today, nailed hastily together like the enormous plastic boxes that line the entrance to Pass-a-Grille today.

Painted garish colors, to catch the harlot's eye, squeezed onto postage-stamp sized lots, bizarre architectural anomalies, rising to the ice cream sherbet skies, the last vestiges of beauty and wonder sold out by corrupt politicians to the greedy real estate developers.

I return to Land's End. An old fisherman joins me on the last, unclaimed spot, and together we cast out under the mellow golden lights off Land's End. Holy ground.

"Where you from?" I inquire, not really caring.

"Atlanta," he answers, "but originally from here."

"Pass-a-Grille?

"Yeah, I used to live her-20-30 years ago. Hardly recognize it. Just like Atlanta. Traffic, congestion- Overcrowded…

The winds of change ripple the water like a jilted lover, as the bells toll in the distance and the first stars sprinkle the sky. The big shore places from across the bay stand dark and empty, silent sandcastles, a few scattered lights left on as a red carnation blooms in one high cathedral window, the reflection of the setting sun, refracted off the water. I stand and watch the last embers of daylight as they fade into twilight and darkness falls. It flickers once, like a distant memory on the horizon, sputters, then burns out like a votive candle left on the altar of some long forgotten dream.

20 Of Fisherman And Fools

One such fisherman, the bane of my fishing existence, was Fisherman Slim. He even wore a nametag as if to prove to everyone that he was a real fisherman. He had the semi-sniveling, awfully officious, self-important air of a petty administrator with the Chamber of Commerce or a small-time PR person at a local beach hotel. His bright, insincere smile seemed to shout, "let me make your day."

He wore a fisherman's hat and vest, properly packed with lures and artificials, with a few fishing flies thrown in to enhance the impression I suppose, although I never saw him try fly-fishing. His name tag read: Fisherman Slim. Just in case anyone missed that fact.

I noticed him watching me one day as I landed fish after fish, all big Snook. I caught them because I had paid my dues, studied the terrain at low tide and understood where and when to fish the high tides. I couldn't shake the suspicion that he was sizing up the spot, like a robber baron, ready to move in for the plunder.

My suspicions were correct. The next day, when I arrived at my usual spot, there he was, seven or eight poles spread out along the wall, fishing as if he owned the spot. Because his rigs were set up everywhere there was a patch of ground to fish, there was no place for me to fish without tripping over one of his rigs or fouling my line in one of his.

I must confess he looked the part of the master fisherman at first, and I admit, even though I was mistrustful, I was impressed. I mean—he had it down. Mr. Fisherman all the way. Yet when it came to fish, I began to notice he rarely caught any.

I knew this spot was loaded with Snook, and so did he now, not because he had a practiced eye, but because he had seen me catch them there, but the finer points eluded him. He just threw everything at them at once—using all eight rigs. Usually, however, he brought the wrong bait at the wrong time, or he fished the in the wrong place along the wall. He rarely appeared during the solunars and barely bothered to look into the water, with his expensive sunglasses, to see what bait was swimming in front of his eyes.

Once in a while he got lucky and hooked a Snook, but he rarely landed it. It would swim into the rocks and snag him or his knot would break.

I could hear him screaming and cursing, making excuses, blaming everyone but himself. It was fun to watch him catch his line on the rocks, and thinking he had a big fish on, become terribly excited, only to realize he was helplessly snagged.

He would grab his knife and cut the line, leaving a long, tangled tail of line in the water, instead of taking the time to climb down into the rocks and cut the line short, thus sparing other fishermen the grief of getting tangled up in his eight line and leaders.

When he did land a Snook, he would yank it up over the wall, and let it thrash about on the pavement, ensuring its death at his hands. He would then hold the fish vertically for someone to take his photograph, crushing its vital organs. Although he let the fish go, he threw them back in from the height of the seawall, through his ignorance, probably critically wounding it every time. It would swim erratically away, falling toward the bottom where it would eventually die.

During the summer we fished together from the wall, Snook were out of season because they were spawning in the channel and the big females were laying their eggs.

In a futile attempt to show him how to keep this great game fish alive, I showed him how to jump off the wall and release the fish while it was still in the water. After a hard fight, you hold the Snook by the tail and gently pull it back and forth through the water, letting the water flow through its gills to revive it. Only then, do you let it go.

If you want to take a photo, hold it under the belly with one hand and grasp it in the mouth with the other, it will lie as gentle as a lamb.

Try to pick it up any other way and it will thrash about. Touch its gills and they will slice your fingers, as they are razor sharp. Treat her gently; let her live to lay her eggs and fight again another day. If she dies millions of Snook eggs die with her.

He continued, however, doing the same thing he had always done, willfully ignorant.

The sin of pride was Fisherman Slim's worst fault—he knew it all. He loved to boast and brag about his fishing prowess. I mean he had all the right gear. And didn't his name-tag say he was a fisherman?

It was his habit to constantly inform me how to fish. As I fished from the wall and walked along with the current to keep my line parallel, he kept up a running commentary, informing me what would and would not work. As we fished side by side, he would provide little pointers, tips from Slim's tacklebox.

I wanted to throw him in the water.

He worked as a bartender in a Tiki Hut at a popular beach hotel, and fancied himself a bit of a local fishing guide. A legend in his own mind. He would bring tourists, by the dozen from the hotel where he was employed, to the once secret Snook Wall, where I lived and fished every day, and which I considered sacred ground.

It became a kind of Disneyworld of Snook-dom.

The tourists never caught anything either, but he liked to show off to them, and soon, thanks to Slim and the monster Snook I was catching every day, the wall became an attraction. Tourist Grand Central, lines and hooks flying, people walking up and down the wall after me, Slim orchestrating the entire procession.

That was the worst part.

Then one day he began to tell me how to walk the wall. I told him flatly that I lived here and knew every inch of terrain along that wall. I had earned it. He and his tourist minions only watched and copied everything they saw me doing. As an observer of nature, one day at low tide I noticed something, which at high tide was virtually invisible: a shallow shelf ran perpendicular to the wall on which I was fishing every day. This shelf ran from north to south, from the bench at 3rd Avenue to the other bench beneath the palm tree at 2nd Ave, a distance of about 35-45 yards.

There was a bay with a little beach. Curious, I jumped down and waded along the shelf, up to my knees to discover the shelf funneled into a narrow channel, which lay down current, where I knew from studying the habitats of Snook they would be laying in wait. Snook prefer to ambush their prey. They would be holding steady, noses facing into the current, pointed north, schools of hungry, spawning Snook.

Since Snook are an opportunistic predator and like to ambush their prey, I reasoned that a fisherman casting his line up-current, north of the bench, would present his bait to be funneled naturally along this shelf until it practically swam right into the fish's mouth. The strike zone! From there you could fight the fish down to the beach and land it on the shore, still in the water. It was perfect.

I also knew, because the Old Salt had told me, that if I used a light circle hook, with a small, split-shot, the shrimp would not drop too fast to the bottom, but would flutter in the mid-level of the water column, right where the Snook were waiting. I guessed, quite correctly, that to make the bait swim naturally, I would have to walk it down the seawall with the current, keeping my line out, parallel to the wall, and drop it precisely right in front of their noses.

That is how I caught my second big Snook. I out-smarted him. It was gray and overcast that day, nobody on the wall. I cast out and let the current take it—wham! Just like that my line was running out, and I almost pitched, head over heels, into the sea. The big Snook came up out of the water and deep inside I knew that he was mine this time. I had his number. I raced along the wall, reeling him in, and leapt off, fighting him down to the beach. I brought him in and landed him on the shore. It felt wonderful, a dream fulfilled. This time it was not luck, but skill. After that it became almost easy.

If he had asked I would have told Fisherman Slim how to catch Snook here, but he never asked. He was too self-absorbed to notice. He would drive up in his SUV, a dozen poles hanging from a rack, park at the curb and step out like he owned the place. He would then thoughtlessly proceeded to lay out these poles at intervals propped up against the seawall, so that I, or any other fisherman, was forced to watch my step or trip over each one as I tried to walk my bait down the wall. His many poles came with a variety of useless hardware attached: bobbers, sinkers, swivels, latches, trinkets and trifles, a bauble for every occasion. It was an obstacle course.

Sloane be nimble, Sloane be quick, watch Sloane jump over Slim's fishing stick.

. The problem was, he just left the lines to drift, which they did in the rushing current, straight back to shore, where the bait lay lifeless on the sand in a foul, tangled mess, which, when I was busy landing my own fish, I had to watch out for lest I too run afoul of his lines and lose my fish or worse-trip and fall into the water.

As I attempted to make my way down the wall, Slim never moved, nor gave way, to me- the man with the fish on—I always had to jump off and walk around him, then maneuver through the obstacle course he had laid out for me.

A few times in my excitement as I struggled with a big fish, I did trip over his various assorted poles, and once I lost a big Snook because I fell.

That was the last straw. I waited for my opportunity. One day it arrived.

As we walked along, he one way, me another, he had the nerve one day to tell me to move. I was in his way!

"I live here!" I snarled, my eyes bent toward him like daggers. "And I've had enough!" I informed him with a dark and dangerous glower. "You had better get out of my way!"

I like to believe at that moment he recognized why I had spent years in Anger Management, and for a brief illuminated instant, even in his dim semi-troglodyte, sub-human consciousness he must've comprehended that I was not going to take a Time Out on this one.

He stepped aide, and I walked around him.

We were never on good terms after that.

Some people are so selfish and self-centered, so dim-witted, thick, dense and obtuse, they have no idea of what other people think. It's as if no one else exists.

One memorable occasion, however, changed everything; I found myself, the quiet unassuming fisherman, thrust into the spotlight.

He brought a tourist with him, of course. Slim rarely fished alone; he desired a witness to his attest to his fishing prowess, preferably one with a camera.

Trouble was neither Slim nor the tourist were catching anything, while I was shouting with joy as I pulled in one big Snook after another.

A photographer took my picture and later published it in the paper.

They stood in one spot, while I wandered, what must've seemed eccentrically up and down the wall catching fish after fish.

Even though they were seeing it with their own eyes, they could not understand what was happening. I was pulling in fish right under their noses.

Finally, the tourist walked over to me and said," I've come a long way for this, and whatever you're using seems to be working, so could you let me in on it?'

"What's the matter, can't Fisherman Slim help you?" I taunted, fed up with Slim and his daily obstacle course.

"So far-you're the only one here who seems to be catching fish."

"That's because I know where they are," I said. "And what and why they're biting."

"You're a local?" He quickly surmised.

"Yeah. I live here. I know the waters, and the fish."

Long ago I learned to listen to the locals," he said. "I'd really appreciate your help." . He wanted to catch a Snook bad, but his rig was loaded with hardware and the wrong bait at the wrong time. Fisherman Slim, the fisherman, had rigged him up of course.

"You'll never catch one with all that stuff on your line," I said.

I liked this man. He was honest and straightforward. He humbled himself to ask for my help, something the Snook Whisperer had said I was obliged to confer upon whosoever asked in the correct spirit.

"OK." I agreed.

What do I do?" He inquired.

"Simple. Take everything off, start over."

"What? I've got the best on now."

"And what have you caught with it so far?" I asked, behind a Cheshire-cat smile.

"I see your point."

"OK. Line to line. And try a new bait."

"Tim said they'd be biting on greenbacks," he jibbed.

"I see," I said. "and he's right. Sometimes they do," I answered.

"But not today" he correctly surmised.

"Not today."

"Why?"

"Because they are almost human, and they like variety. At this moment they prefer shrimp. But not just any shrimp, jumbos. Simple: Big bait, big fish. Tomorrow it might be pinfish, after that, greenies or grunts. You have to adapt to what they want."

"I'm a businessman. It's just like business. Give the customer what he wants and you will ensure success."

"Exactly!"

By this time Fisherman Slim had ambled over. He did not enjoy losing a client to me, and he showed his displeasure.

"What's going on here?" He demanded to know.

"Nothing!" smiled the tourist. "But with his help, that's about to change."

Fisherman Slim shot me a glance, as if to say, who do you think you are? I'm the fisherman here, can't you read my name tag?

"Oh, that's right—you're Fisherman Slim. I forgot, " I mocked..

"What do you think you're doing?" Fisherman Slim asked me coldly.

"Showing a man how to catch a fish," I answered matter of factly.

"If I may." I unsheathed my knife.

The tourist nodded, granting me permission to do as I desired.

As the Snook Whisperer had done, I cut the tourist's short 12 inch mono leader and shiny silver hook from Slim's rig, and spooled out a 36 inch fluro leader from my own roll, tying it directly to his main line, then tied the leader directly to one of my darker light-wire, circle hooks, as the Old Salt had taught me. I hooked a jumbo shrimp through the horn and handed the rod back to the tourist.

"Try that."

"Thanks," he said and cast out.

"Walk it down," I suggested.

"It's better to stay in one spot," Slim replied. "And use a variety of rigs." He had, as usual, several splayed out along the wall, none of which was bent double at the moment.

"All you need is one if you know where the Strike Zone is, and it's rigged correctly. Now walk it down," I repeated. "Keep your line straight out, parallel to the shore. Be ready."

"I've stayed in one spot long enough," said the tourist. He sauntered away along the wall. Halfway down—his rod bent double.

I smiled innocently, Fisherman Slim's eyes burning a hole in the back of my head.

The tourist looked back at me in astonishment as his drag began to sing a sweet song. He had been standing in one spot for an hour and caught nothing, now in a few seconds he had a big one on.

Fisherman Slim did not speak, yet he watched every move. As I walked by, balancing on the wall, I came face to face with him

"Excuse me," I said politely. I could not keep the smugness out of my voice.

Down on the beach, the tourist was busy landing the Snook; I felt my rod bend double and my drag start to sing.

Fisherman Slim was still in my way. I could see his rods laid out beyond me, blocking my path.

This time I squared my shoulders and made him move out of my way and as I walked down the wall, I kicked his useless pieces of shit, the incorrectly rigged rods and reels out of my way as I went, fighting a large, leaping Snook.

They went clattering all over the pavement.

I heard Fisherman Slim curse me to my back, and I smiled inwardly.

It was still all about him and his ego, but on this day I owned the wall!

"Fish on!" I shouted as I joined the tourist down on the beach. We fought our fish side by side, laughing like children. When we brought them in, we hi-fived each other with child-like glee.

"Nice fish," I smiled, happy to have helped him achieve his dream.

"I've wanted to catch one of these my whole life," he said. "Thank you."

"My pleasure."

He reached into his wallet and handed me a hundred dollar bill. "You ought to be a guide," he said.

Up on the wall Fisherman Slim looked down on us, his best PR smile pasted on his face. "Nice fish," he tired to act charitable, but the smile was as fake as he was.

I waved the Hamilton in the air.

Slim was not a happy fisherman, but I was. Ha!

21 A Fish Story: In Memory Of Elizabeth Reed

It may be an apocryphal story. It was told to me by a fisherman, a group notorious for telling fictitious anecdotes, yet it has the ring of truth. There were two witnesses that day, a doctor and his son, both neighbors. The fact it was narrated by a complete stranger is all the more intriguing because he had no reason to lie.

He was an aging, non-descript hippie who plopped himself down beside me on the sea wall in Pass-a-Grille, facing east.

He told me a story I'll never forget, an alleged confessional from the soul of a great modern songwriter.

"Ever heard the song In Memory of Elizabeth Reed?" He inquired.

"Sure," I said. "The Allman Brothers. Idlewild South—classic southern rock."

His long, silver-gray hair ruffled slightly as his washed-out blue eyes scanned the horizon. He seemed a little inebriated, although he might just have been in high spirits. It was difficult to tell.

"Well, you know how it's always been something of a secret, the stuff of rock and roll legend?"

He looked at me as if to underscore his point. "No one ever heard of Elizabeth Reed, so who was this mystery woman, and why was such a great song named after someone no one ever heard of?

Everyone's always wondered where the original song-writer, who shall remain anonymous, and who shall be known hereafter by his initials, DB, came up with the name, and what was the story behind it."

The Old Hippie smiled. "Rolling Stone, the magazine, or any other publication would give a fortune to know what I'm about to tell you, but just because you're a fellow fisherman, I'm going tell you."

"On my 39th birthday, my sister got me a backstage pass to an Allman Brothers concert. She knows someone in the band. So there I was hanging out backstage with the roadies, just sitting there minding my own business, when in walks DB, the writer of the song, Elizabeth Reed, and sits down, and starts doing illegal substances right in front of us, chasing them with a shot of Jack Daniels straight from the bottle.

"Hey! Pay attention," he growled in that raspy, whiskey-soaked voice. "I'm about to tell you something, boy! "I'm tired of keeping it a secret--the time has come lay the truth bare."

"What?" I asked him.

"Elizabeth Reed: The real story."

"The roadies dropped whatever it was they were doing and gathered 'round. Now you know when roadies, who've seen and heard everything, get interested, you're about to hear something special, so I sat there waiting. I wasn't disappointed."

"It was like this…" DB began… "Me and my best friend's wife, we had a thing for each other. She smote my heart. I was in love with her so bad it hurt, and she with me, but we couldn't say anything. Would've broken up the band. Caused a lot of hard feelings. One day, we went out for a walk in the woods, just holding hands, you know.

Young, innocent, naive. Happy to be together. She was so beautiful; I loved her, but it was a forbidden love. Told her I was gonna write a song for her."

"She got really excited, wanted to know if I was going to name it after her?"

"I told her flat out, I can't name it after you, baby," it's a love song."

DB chuckled at the memory, and chugged the bottle straight back. "Courage," he husked, remembering, a troubled look in his dark, somber eyes.

"Anyway, we came to this graveyard, see. Out in the woods in a grove of Live Oaks, hung with Spanish Moss. Middle of nowhere. It's winter—cold, crisp, gray day, a hint of snow in the air: wind scattering fallen leaves all around us. She thought it was romantic."

"We walked along, through the rows of graves, up to our ankles in the leaves; I remember she was wearing a scarf, which she wrapped around my neck to keep me warm." DB paused, either for dramatic effect or to consider the efficacy of his next words. There was no turning back now.

"I gave her a hug. One thing led to another. A hug led to a kiss, a kiss led to--we didn't have a blanket, so I lay her down across a tombstone off to the side of the graveyard, and we made love. Wild, passionate love, the kind that takes your breath away. For the first and the last time."

"Jesus!" One of the roadies uttered beneath his breath.

"Yeah," I agreed, that's quite a story."

"Oh, but there's more. The Hippie added conspiratorially. "This is the best part."

"When we were done," DB sighed, "and we had consummated our love, I rolled over, wiped the sweat out of my eyes, and looked up.

There was this name carved on the headstone above us: In Memory of Elizabeth Reed."

"Wow! Now that's a fish story!" I laughed out loud.

"The sad thing is," DB confided, "no one could ever know the song I wrote, Elizabeth Reed, was really about the love I had for the wife of my best friend."

Sadness lay upon his face, and from somewhere in the shadow of his eyes, a light had gone out. "For her and only her."

DB sighed heavily. "Everyone always wondered where the name came from, but it was our secret. I poured my heart and soul into that song, and no one ever knew—until now. Listen close, you can hear it in my guitar—passion, longing, burning desire- and pain and regret."

The story took me back to my own doomed love affair, destined to end unhappily ever after. We all have that one true love– the one we can't forget. I told the Old Hippie about a girl from Nantucket with eyes like wildflowers, blue-bonnets, swaying in the breeze, on a hill in a meadow, yet they were not happy eyes, but rather filled with a kind of shy New England reticence, like the oblique slant of autumnal light, the Lenten austerity of winter stars. Her honey-golden hair, tinted with tiny wisps of auburn embers, shone incandescent in the sunshine, sparking into flame; while her face, as fay as the fabled Sphinx of Egypt, held a smattering of freckles diagonally criss-crossing the bridge of her nose and cheekbones. She was the girl next door, who remained, ironically out of reach.

I kissed her high on a crag above the ocean, somewhere along Old Cliff Road in Sconsett, the whitecaps sweeping in off the gray Atlantic in long, rolling swells, breaking like peals of thunder as they hurled against the bluffs below us. It was the end of summer, and I was saying goodbye forever, though I did not know it at the time; I can still hear the sound of my heart breaking with the waves on the rocks.

"I guess everyone has their story," the Old gray-pony-tailed Hippie mused.

Yeah," I agreed, my eyes straying toward the horizon.

"Well, that's about it," the Aging Hippie rose to depart. "Oh, DB told me one last thing that night: 'Said he saw her years later. She ran up to him and gave him a big hug; and the years fell away,' he said. "She stood there as beautiful as ever and he knew in his heart, he was still in love with her. She told him how she re-lived that day every time she heard the song. Their song. In Memory of Elizabeth Reed."

"Every time I play it, I play it for you," DB confessed, his whiskey-ravaged voice, caressing the memory. "And every time I think of what might've been."

The story reads like a fable, one of those timeless tales, in which a fisherman opens the mouth of his catch to discover a lost treasure, only in this case, the riches I extract are a universal insight into the affairs of men and women of love and inevitably- loss. Surely it's no accident it was conceived on a tombstone in a graveyard in the dead of winter, for everyone holds a special memory, which lays bare their inner-most secret longings and desires, and which most of us keep to ourselves, until the old familiar scent of perfume, wafts from across a room, or we re-visit a place from the distant past, with a meaning only we can begin to comprehend—in a lonely graveyard amid the Live Oaks, or high on a bluff above the ocean, in the sound of a timeless love-song spilling out of the radio.

The self-destructive drug and alcohol abuse, the meaningless one night stands in between, the loneliness and temptations of the road—a physical consummation of forbidden love on the tombstone of a woman long since dead, once upon a winter's day- out of the pathos of death and love, a beautiful song emerges, spreads it wings and takes flight once more if only in imagination, like a butterfly sprung from a chrysalis: As time goes by--In Memory of Elizabeth Reed.

22 Swimming With The Sharks: In Hollywood

One night I had a dream that changed everything. I was a black man, hanging out with the late, great Jimi Hendrix, the most gifted guitarist who ever lived. We were living on the streets, and I kind of got the feeling what it would be like to be black and a genius. It was to be misunderstood.

The first time I heard a song by Jimi Hendrix. I was walking through the woods to my girlfriend's house. I was listening to a small red transistor radio. The Beatles, "I Want to Hold Your Hand," was playing. I switched stations, this time Elvis' Blue Suede Shoes. I thumbed the dial on the side and tuned into another broadcast and another world: this time something astonishingly unaccustomed caught my ear. A broadcast from another realm it seemed: the opening notes of "All Along the Watchtower," the high wailing notes filled the silent spaces of the forest—like God's throbbing heartbeat, and the landscape around me changed.

By the time I got to my girlfriend's house, I was a different person. Something happened that day.

I forgot all about it, until decades later I had the dream and I heard those haunting notes again. That night I truly became experienced. The dream was so real it touched me profoundly, in a way that as a white person I could never fully understand.

"Tell them what it's like," Jimi said. "Tell them my story. The story of who I was. A man with hopes and dreams who found the courage to fly with a broken wing. And tell them about my last song."

Then I awoke. I didn't even know Jimi had written a last song—the mythic last song of blues geniuses, but after some research, I found something unusual. Upon his death, September 18th, 1970 at the Samarkind Hotel, after taking nine packets of sleeping powder, out of a pack of ten, in the pocket of his old coat, Jimi had indeed penned a last song- The Story of Life: Slow. About Jesus. So there was a last song—and he wanted it known. Jimi Hendrix, Jesus Freak.

I wrote a beautiful, idealistic screenplay about Jimi Hendrix and his last song, and sent it out. It was pure myth. The hype found in all the books.

Nothing happened until a year later when Jimi's brother, LH let it be known he liked my script, but he wanted to tell the real, untold story. Straight from the horse's mouth. He told me, indirectly about Jimi's early life. He countered the official story of Jimi's father Al, of whom it is said bought the guitar virtuoso, his first guitar. In actuality, Jimi's Aunti lent Al the money to purchase Jimi's first guitar. A small yet significant detail.

Also according to LH, Jimi Hendrix, guitar legend, stuttered until his early teens. Barely able to express himself verbally, Jimi let his guitar do the talking for him. Upon their mother Lucille's untimely death, Al did not allow the boys to attend their mother's funeral, igniting dark hints of a love affair, and Jimi's true paternity.

I'll never forget the last words Jimi said in the dream. "please, put my last song in your story," he asked, ever polite. "It was never recorded. It was a big dream of mine. A cry of love."

Because he left no will, and his estate is a tangled mess to this day, his last song serves as a kind of last will and testament.

To me the lyrics reveal this great artist's spiritual side, an artist whose reputation has been defamed and dragged through the mud, called a psychedelic Uncle Tom, a burned-out drug freak, to many the sound of his guitar, a mere echo of his drug-induced state, the halo of his afro, a corona seen through the purple haze of LSD.

But he was much more than that. He was a man of sorrows and acquainted with grief. A redeemer. Born to poverty he learned to play on a beat-up one-string Ukulele his father may have found in the trash on one of his landscaping jobs; Jimi learned quickly, however, that if he played that one string from the heart, the other end was not attached to the tuning peg of his guitar, it was strung out across the universe, and he could make it sing like twelve.

Lucille, his mother, a beautiful woman whom Jimi idolized, died young and was buried in an unmarked grave; he was not allowed to attend her funeral and longed for her the rest of his life; he remained withdrawn and isolated, loving few, trusting none even as he basked in the international spotlight of the world's stage.

By all accounts of those closest to him, and I have talked with Jimi's brother and personally traveled to Nashville, Tennessee, to talk to Billy Cox, the one true companion to whom Jimi turned after the Experience broke up, Jimi was a hard-working, deeply humble, spiritual man. His work ethic was prodigious. He was somewhere playing guitar every night of his adult life, learning as he said to go a little further out on that one string. Yet those in whose care he labored and whom he made rich, betrayed him in the end.

They overworked, underpaid and undervalued the man-child with the God-like gift.

It was his simple child-like faith, his belief in his music, which kept his heart pure to the end, Billy said. Upon Jimi's death, the highest paid performer in the world, had $14 dollars in his bank account.

He did not die of a drug overdose as the myths expound. Exhausted, worn-out from touring, he took some sleeping packets. All he wanted was a good night's sleep.

9 little packets in all, of a higher dosage than he was used to taking in the States, which, when combined with alcohol, a little wine he had had for dinner, affected him adversely, ultimately killing him in his sleep.

Yet the number 9 has implications. It's was Jimi's number, the mystic numeral. One has to wonder why he took 9. There were ten packets in all, so the mystery only deepens. But the ability to see below the surface that fishing teaches, taught me to look deeper.

Dead at 27, according to the autopsy report, from a combination of sleeping aids and alcohol, which proved fatal. Drowned in his own vomit. The woman by his side that night—a virtual stranger did nothing until it was too late. Thus the most brilliant and beloved musician of his age, perhaps any age, died like a dog, alone and broke, tired and weary, practically destitute. Yet his cry of love continues, and lives on in his music.

I took me a year but I finally finished the new screenplay based on LH's insights into his brother; I entitled it "Jimi Hendrix: Cry of Love," in honor of the dream.

I sent it out to my partner in Hollywood, and we got some nibbles, but mostly, like the little fish, it was a waste of time. Yet I knew I had the right bait and I persisted. I sent it to Billy Cox. He invited us to come up to Nashville, where he was the proprietor of a pawn shop, and we spoke at length about the Jimi he knew, the man not the myth.

It was he who told me about the betrayals. The Professor, he called me. He trusted me enough to share a few insider secrets, which I included in the script.

I re-wrote it once more and sent it back out, where it fell into the hands of a Producer, now residing in Hollywood. I came home and heard nothing for more than a year, until the call came, oddly enough, at the precise moment that my dream of a big fish—my first Snook-came true, and it came in tune, as Jimi would have it, to the sound of my cell phone ringing in time to the music of my drag singing as the line played out with the Snook on the other end.

"Hello. This is L. F.," the voice at the other end stated. "You're going to be a hit-maker. The Shakespeare of Screenwriters."

"What?" I asked astonished. This was a bolt out of the blue.

"I want to turn your screenplay into a film. I think it's awesome. I don't want to change a word." He had the first idealistic version—before Jimi's brother.

There I stood, openmouthed, with my dream fish in my hand, and the culmination of my biggest dream on the telephone. Both on the same day at the same moment.

"Sure." I laughed, kissed the Snook on the mouth and let it go. Once again a Snook was bound up with my destiny.

"I'll be in touch," he said and hung up. It was a very happy time. I was a fisherman and a writer. I had a screenplay making waves in Hollywood, a Snook on the end of my hook, and my fishing book was coming out.

Meanwhile another big-shot, a real estate magnate in Seattle, C. D., got a hold of it, read it, and stopped production of the film he was working on.

He came to a meeting with a ten page contract in his pocket: 1% of the budget, or about $600,000, plus one hundred thousand dollars down to purchase the screenplay. He seemed obsessed with Jimi Hendrix. He had purchased Jimi's childhood home and saved it from being razed.

He sued Jimi's half-sister, Janie to get Leon, Jimi's legitimate brother, back in the will, but the Judge upheld Al's last will and testament. In fairness, Janie had nursed Al in his last days on his death bed, so she did in fact, deserve some consideration. But to cut Jimi's brother out of the will entirely—I don't think Jimi would've approved.

Overnight it seemed I had two competing producers competing to buy my work. But which one should I promote? The real one or the myth?

To make matters worse, rumors swirled that another writer had re-written my script and passed it off as his own.

My partner called one night late, his voice manic, half-insane. "It's up to three million dollars now. It's no longer about the script, it's about the deal."

I tried to talk to him, but could not get him to explain his enigmatic words.

"You'll see," he said. "This is big!"

Needless to say, I got no sleep that night. Try as I might, I could not close my eyes.

I was swimming with the big fish now- in shark infested waters! And there was blood in the water. My days from fishing for big sharks came in handy as I recalled the lessons learned. Always hold the shark by the tail to avoid its teeth. Use a gaff to grab it before it grabs you.

I decided to play them off against each other. Make the big fish fight for it if they wanted my screenplay. That way I had them by the tail. Let them bite each other not me.

We hired an entertainment attorney to represent us. That's the way to hold them with the gaff. Put it in writing. That's the lesson of

Hollywood. So many people promise you everything. Most of it is talk. Get it in writing—that's your gaff to hold them.

Big fish, remember will always have one last run. In the end it was a little like that classic short story, "The Lady or the Tiger," in which a man faces two doors.

Behind one is a beautiful lady, behind the other—a tiger. The question is which is which? The woman who loves him comes to him by night and whispers the answer in his ear. But is she jealous, not wanting him to have the lady or loyal, not wanting to see him die at the claws of the tiger?

At the conclusion to the story the man opens the door. We never learn what comes out of it—nor is that important. What's important is the choice.

23 Today's The Day

JULY 10TH. 2005. It's been a year since the fight with the big Snook on the jetty. Then nothing really. I almost hung up my rod and reel for good, or so I thought.

Today I was fishing between two other fishermen, who were just packing up.

I overheard their talk of leaving just as the fish I knew from the coming of the Solurnars, were about to start biting.

"Let's go, there's nothing biting here," quoth the Fisherman #1 in his infinite wisdom.

"Hey, bud," the Fisherman #2 yells at me and Fisherman Slim. "You guys are wasting your time. Been here for hours. Haven't caught a damned thing."

"That's about to change" I answer, trying not to sound too cocky.

"That's right," chimes in Fisherman Slim. Yeah, he's still around.

"Yeah, right," scoffs Fisherman #2.

Suddenly my pole bends double; I pull in a large Snook, release it, re-bait and cast out. My drag begins to sing as my line heads out.

"JeeZus! What the hell?" Fisherman #2 stares at me. But he doesn't do anything. Just stares.

"I told you," I say. "The Solurnars."

Fisherman #1 looks at me like I'm nuts. "The what?"

I can't believe he calls himself a fisherman, even wears a little nametag proclaiming himself as one, yet has never heard of the Solunars, but when I try to explain his eyes glaze over.

I hook up another jumbo shrimp and whisk it out, then walk it down the wall, from the bench to the trash can, between 2nd Avenue. I stop just under the palm and allow the hook to dangle in front of where I know a school of Snook lay just beneath the surface.

Suddenly, he's back. "What are you doing?" Fisherman Slim asks.

"I'm going to catch a big one."

His look tells me all I need to know.

"You have to keep your line in one place to catch a big Snook." Tips from Fisherman Slim. Problem is, as usual he's not catching any.

"Fish on!" I yell as my pole bends double and I begin to crank the reel.

"How the hell did you do that!" Fisherman #1 wants to know.

On the next high tide I tested what I had learned, and sure enough, it worked like magic. I caught ten Snook that day, in fast and furious action, one after another, while fisherman all around me caught nothing.

There is an unwritten code among fisherman that you do not intrude upon another fisherman's territory, and most were respectful of this time-honored tradition. Except for one-Fisherman Slim, the bane of my fishing existence…

Usually I wait until the Solurnar is over before I quit the spot. I would depart and watch as the other fishermen on the wall ran to my location between the benches, but the Solurnars were over—and the fish were going to stop biting.

Fisherman #1 saw the action, but just sat there, staring down at the rocks. He was using the wrong presentation, but unaware or worse, did not care anymore. And he's fishing on the rocks, something I long ago learned to avoid.

Every once in a while a small fish takes him down into the rocks and he loses everything, hook, line and sinker, and has to start all over.

A familiar routine. A year and a half earlier that was me. I feel sorry for him, and decide to divulge my secrets.

"Try walking it down I tell him and keep your line tight, perpendicular to the wall. That way it looks natural. The Snook are right over here." I point to where the shelf funnels into the channel. Get up and walk it down, keep your line parallel to your body, so he can feel the slightest touch.

He wants to know how I know this?

"I just do." I offer him a large shrimp, because he's using the wrong bait, but he's not listening.

I try again. "I'm not trying to tell you how to fish," I say. "Just trying to show you why and where they are. I live around here. I know."

"Nah. I'll never catch anything," he says and hangs his head, his line drifting listlessly. On closer inspection, I notice the current has borne it to the shore. His hook is literally dragging on the sand.

Too many people live like this man. Neither ready, nor engaged in what's happening. Just drifting with the flow even though the flow is taking them nowhere. If they would only get up and try something different. The signs are all around them. They have eyes, but they refuse to see what is right in front of them. And it's tragic, because it's so easy.

Fisherman #1 has lost all confidence. If he would try one more time…No, he probably wouldn't catch anything even if he did have all the essentials right, because he does not believe he can. What is happening before his eyes doesn't make any sense.

He's been here for hours, and I walk up, throw my line in and begin pulling in one Snook after another, so he has to convince himself it's his bad luck and my good luck.

My drag screams as I reel in yet another big Snook, land him and release him.

"You got some special bait or something," he wonders aloud.

"Just shrimp. Well, no—jumbo shrimp, actually. Snook prefer them large." I've already told him this. Apparently he wasn't listening.

"I'm using cut squid," he added without confidence.

"I know," I say, trying to sound encouraging. I can see the raw, doughy lump, which no self-respecting Snook would touch, dangling from the end of his hook.

"They're hitting on cut squid over next to the bridge; thought they'd be hitting on the same thing here."

Only they're not, and never will be. And it's insane to go on doing what you are doing when you know it is not working, but he only stares at the ground and states matter of factly that he will never catch anything again. Perhaps he never will. I see them everyday, foolish fishermen stuck on the rocks. Too afraid to try something new, even though it may mean the difference between failure and success.

So we persist—day after day, year after year, and the result is always the same. Meanwhile, the fisherman or businessman standing next to you is catching fish after fish, after fish, making money, making his dreams come true.

One of the requirements, in the fulfillment of a big dream, is to keep an open mind, to be prepared to grow and expand, to change direction in mid-stream and find another way that works, until you catch and land your dream. Only the self-delusional will persist in something that never works.

In the midst of this three-penny opera, The Pampano Lady strolled by walking her poodle. She offered to cast her net for me to catch some bait-fish. I gladly comply, and she lifts up a net-ful of Silver Jennys, squirming into my bait-pail.

I hook the Silver Jenny through the nose and cast it out. Another strike! The pole bends double and everyone watches as I rake in another large Snook. All this while Fisherman #1 and #2 cast out on either side of me, neither one catching a thing.

"You've got it down to an art," she smiles. "Like me and my Pompano," and strolls away with her poodle.

Fisherman #2 tosses his cut squid into the sea, and loops his hook through a guide. He has given up in the midst of plenty.

The banquet feast is spread out before him, yet he walks away. He examines my fishing rod and reel: a Loomis GMX, and a Shimano Stella, with which I can outcast and outmaneuver almost anyone. I have upgraded to the best, because I'm serious now. I mean business!

With the new rod and reel fishing becomes effortless; I can feel every nibble on the end of my line, so at the exact moment when the fish bites, I know just when to set the hook. My 30 pound test braided line gives me the assurance that I will not lose a big fish in the heat of battle and the knot I've tied, the confidence to know it will hold when the big one does hit.

"You got some kind of special rig, maybe?" he shrugs, never dreaming how close he is to Snook, nor how far.

"How much it cost ya?"

"Everything!" I say. "But it was worth it. I'd give everything and more to catch big fish."

Fisherman #2 shakes his head. "Maybe it's the fisherman."

"You guys quitting already?" I ask as the other one tries one last time. Yet I know he will catch nothing.

"You have all the luck. Me, I have no luck"

I had to laugh. If only they knew. To them it must've appeared a random stroke of luck that I was catching so many fish, while, standing right beside me, they caught nothing, yet in fact it was quite the opposite; they had good luck if they had only known it, for they were standing next to a fishermen who had learned about luck the hard way, through trial and error, failure and triumph. They were looking for the treasure when they were standing on X marks the spot.

I was just like them, only I was prepared for success not failure. I had the right bait, and the best tackle at the right time; I had merely exhausted all the possibilities. I made my own luck.

With a word I would have given them my hard-won secrets, told them exactly how and where to catch the big ones, but they never asked. So sure were that they would never catch anything. Yet it was there for the asking. It's a mystery to me why so many people prefer to go without, to settle for less, in the midst of plenty, when the riches are spread out before their unseeing eyes.

"I have no luck," they whine. "I'm too poor, I can't do it. "I'll never catch anything."

My favorite saying is a saying of Mel Fisher: Today's the Day. You can visit his museum on Duval Street in Key West: The Mel Fischer Museum.

Mel's the man who spent his life searching for the Atochia, a Spanish Galleon, laden with gold. They called him crazy, delusional, but he held onto his dream with a mantra he repeated every day. "Today's the Day." He persisted, dreaming of the big one, and one day he discovered 400,000,00 dollars worth of gold and precious gems lying buried in the sand.

Like the elusive Snook of my dreams, the treasure was there all along, just waiting for someone who dared to go and find it.

Make your own luck. Today's the day! The American dream is there for one and all. But not for these two fisherman. They gave up too easily. It took Mel Fisher decades to land his big dream, and he lost a son before he finally caught it. I keep my mouth shut and go on fishing and pulling in the big ones right in front of them. They just shrug it off and try again. It's sad really. They're probably still sitting there to this day, fishing on the rocks, using the wrong bait at the wrong time, in the wrong place, cursing their luck, while all around them treasure abounds. Today's the day to go fishing, today's the day to make your dreams come true-today's the day.

24 If Love Were All

Many of the colder winter afternoons, my father and I spent watching old movies. We watched Laural and Hardy, The Marx Brothers, and his favorite, "The Prisoner of Zenda," with Ronald Coleman and Mary Astor. The best of these old films, all had the idea of the noble ideal, a dream large enough to strive for, to sacrifice for—to believe in.

When we first see the hero, Ronald Colemen, (Rudolph) in "The Prisoner of Zenda," Rudolph, is fishing in a trout stream, so I liked him immediately. He is also a double for the king, an arrogant, shallow, self-centered ruler. In a twist of fate, Rudolph must assume the mantle of kingship and take the king's place until the real king can be restored to the throne. In the meantime, the future queen falls for Rudolph because he has suddenly become such a good and humble man. A gentlemen and a fisherman to be sure.

As the plot unfolds, in a dramatic turn of events, Rudolph the counterfeit and Flavia, the queen fall in love, but in the end, the rightful king returns and Rudolph must relinquish his hold on the kingdom and the queen he loves, and go back to the life of an ordinary fisherman. Yet it has been his hand, his steady leadership and sense of common humanity with his subjects which has won the day.

In a tearful goodbye, the queen wants to run away with him, but Rudolph/Ronald Coleman counsels her to stay and to do her duty. In the end, she agrees: "If love were all," she sighs. But duty binds a woman too, Rudolph."

Both are prepared to sacrifice their love for a higher cause, for the honor of the king and the good of the kingdom.

As he takes his leave she asks if she will ever see him again. He turns to her one last time and says, in that romantic never to be forgotten voice," Shan't a man return to the most beautiful woman in the kingdom? A thousand Black Michael's couldn't keep me away. But if I shouldn't you'll be a good queen, you'll do your part…"

"History doesn't always make the right man king," the king's loyal counselor, Sir Aubrey Smith, tells Rudolph at the end as he rides off into the sunset. He has what we call character—the desire to do the right thing at the right time, for the good of all.

So true. All will be right with the world when all fishermen are crowned kings, and all the kings are fishermen.

The noble ideal of honor and self-sacrifice has been almost entirely lost to our generation; we are consumed with ourselves, obsessed with our selfish, self-centered narcissistic culture. Celebrity, good or bad, rules our lives, and we will do anything for our 15 minutes. Indeed, we have sunk so low, that in some quarters, a double homicide, and its surrounding remoras, counts as a path to fame.

The big dream, if it is to be worth anything of true value, must possess an element of sacrifice and character. You must be willing to give up something to gain possession of whatever it is you so desire. The more you give of yourself, the nobler the dream.

"It was better in the old days in River Plaza," my father mused. "Even though we had a depression, world wars, poverty, we had a nobility of spirit. We had heroes with character. We believed in a higher cause, something greater than our selves. You see it only in the soldiers today, like the soldiers of the past.

They are willing to lay down their lives for something-freedom, democracy, the triumph of good over evil. Today, the art, the music, the movies, they've sunk so low, there aren't any heroes anymore. Not in the way we counted heroes."

And sitting there watching those old movies with him, of a cold winter's afternoon, with the sound of Ronald Coleman's voice still ringing in my ears, I have to agree—character counts.

- If love were all.

25 Silver Kings: Lesson Of The Tarpon

One morning, as usual, I was out walking the eastern wall (the Snook Wall) searching for signs of fish. What I saw stunned me. I had jumped a pair of Silver Kings. 10 yards from where I stood, rolling in the clear blue-green water, two Tarpon cavorted, just off shore. Fortunately, or perhaps because I knew enough by now to always be prepared, I had two rods with me, one of them rigged with my invaluable sibiki, so I quickly lowered it down, one eye still on the Tarpon, and hooked a pin-fish.

I slipped my hook through the dorsal and raced down the wall to catch up with the pair of silver kings, praying they would stop and accept my offer.

I jumped off the wall and ran down the beach ahead of them. I wanted to time this perfectly so as not to spook them, but to cast out just in time for the pinfish to sink down in front of their noses.

I timed it perfectly, casting out high and far, knowing the currents in that area would roll it back close to shore, just as they swam by, like a golfer timing a putt on the green, to roll just close enough to the hole to be able to make par.

There was a great thrashing—a giant displacement of water. I had hooked one. It rose up in front of me, the pinfish locked in its immense brute shelf of an acromegalic jaw.

It leapt again and again, high against the white summer clouds, surging skyward to escape the hook in its mouth, its body clearing the water, dancing across the waves, before gravity took over and it fell back on its own momentum with a crash, splitting the seas asunder!

I bowed my head and leaned forward on the beach, in what is called "the bow," so as not to let it throw the hook-- then I let it have it. I set the hook hard-five, six times with all my might, so as to drive the point of the hook home into its iron-clad chin. A Tarpon's jaw is cartilage. Tough and sinewy. The hook almost has to be pounded like a nail into solid oak.

I had a fish on! A big fish on. Then the fun began.

His initial surge nearly pulled me off my feet; the power was incredible as it dragged me down the beach at a run my rod and reel stretched out before me, the line un-spooling in a long continuous wail. I had seen fishing guides on TV catch Tarpon on relatively light tackle, so I knew it could be done, but having one on yourself is quite different from sitting in your Lazy-Boy watching someone else fight a Silver King. I had fifty pound braid on and a fifty pound leader, so as long as I stayed close and did not allow it to spool me, I had a fighting chance.

My adrenalin was pumping. Cold sweat ran down my back. My mouth had gone bone dry. I buried my thumb in the spool to slow the fish down—it did not slow down. Then I tried palming it- still it did not slow down. It merely continued to swim out to sea, un-spooling line as it went. I followed it out into the water, up to my knees, then deeper to my waist and yanked back again and again—hard. Nothing, it just kept swimming.

Fish On!

I ducked under the dock at Land's End and ran with it down the little sandy beach toward the jetty in the west. It showed no signs of slowing down. I wasn't about to stop this fish anytime soon, so I devised a strategy, to think about what I would do if it took me all the way to the jetty. Endurance was key.

To keep the Tarpon from running out all my line and breaking me off, I had to stay as close to it as I could, which meant, I was going to have to climb the granite rocks, fight it along those rocks, climb up onto the jetty, fish it from the rail, pull or persuade it somehow to circle around the jetty, instead of running straight out to sea, and fight it back down the other side of the rocks, to the beach, where I could fight it from the shore-line all the way from St. Pete to Clearwater if I had to.

The fish had other ideas.

When jumping a Tarpon, especially a large one, it's best to have a boat, to run it down because it pulls mightily—it will pull a boat out to sea or beneath bridge pilings. I was on foot, and it was pulling me out to sea. I was in up to my neck.

I once saw a fisherman in a boat jump a Tarpon, right off the jetty where I was now heading, and because his anchor-line got fouled with the buoy, he could not pull it up and chase the Tarpon down. Consequently, it yanked his boat from stern to bow, this way and that, until he had to cut his line and let it go.

The Tarpon is a powerhouse—the fullback of fish.

I had to somehow get that Tarpon to change direction, only by a degree, so I could steer it toward the jetty, then down the beach north instead of south toward the 90 foot channel at Eggmont Key. I did not think I could swim that far, although I'm sure the fish could've dragged me.

The Tarpon was not cooperating. So I settled for merely slowing it down until I could convince it to change its course. I used every trick

I know-I palmed the spool, tightening it down by degrees, then trying to go "down and dirty." Nothing worked. Finally I just waited-endured, showed the fish I wasn't giving up.

Just as my head was about to go under water, I held the rod above my head, I felt an imperceptible slowing of the fish. Instantly I yanked hard in the direction of the jetty. It changed course slightly. Next I backed out of the water, reeling in line, toward the rocks on the southern end of the jetty. I climbed the rocks, one hand holding onto the rod, the other feeling my way along so as not to trip and fall. Then I ran along the rocks, reeling in line as I ran, as fast and as far as I could, until the iron railing at the farthermost western tip of the jetty, stopped me dead in my tracks.

I had gained back some line. I decided to go for broke. I was tiring, but so was the fish. I screwed the drag down tight, as tight as it would go and heaved the fishes' weight, sideways, down and dirty toward the north shore and the beach.

To my surprise it turned.

I then climbed down the rocks on the north side of the jetty and fought it down onto the beach. My strategy was working, so far.

I worked it down the beach a ways, about 35 yards from the jetty, almost directly in front of my house, and prayed it would not turn back, but it did.

Back toward the jetty, and I too went back again with it, climbing up the rocks, fighting it to the iron railing, then stopping the fish and repeating the process all over again.

The crowd that had gathered, walking the beach with me, had all but vanished.

And the fun along with it. I was tired now. My back, my arms, my legs ached. I no longer cared weather or not I caught this fish; I longed to stop and go home and get something to eat. Maybe take a hot bath. Have a Maker's Mark with ginger ale and a drop of pure rainwater. I was hungry, tired, thirsty—and worst of all-bored.

So was the crowd. Most had left by now; only a few remained.

Back and forth we went, up and down the beach, then along the rocks, back to the jetty-once all the way back to the southern-side of the rocks on the jetty and back again. Like a yo-yo on a string. It would take line out; I'd reel it back in, for about an hour and a half. I fought that fish way down the beach before I finally brought it in close enough to grab the leader to pull the tired fish in, but then I felt the line go slack- I reeled in. The tarpon had straightened out the hook- it was not even bent at an angle-just a long straight shank of solid steel. The big fish was gone, but I had touched the leader, so it was OK.

Gasping for breath in the hot humid summer air, I was actually elated it was all over. I had endured and overcome many obstacles in the fight: hunger, thirst, boredom. It had been hard work. To fulfill your dreams you must endure.

And watch out for the boredom—it's the nastiest pit-fall of all, because it robs you of desire- you want to willingly give up, slack off, let it go. You can't. If you want it—you have to earn it- to fight for it. The dream has to be won. Endurance: that's the lesson of the Tarpon.

26 Bluewater: Lesson Of The Marlin

Arrows of light refract off blue water like consummately cut diamonds dancing so bright it hurts my eyes. I'm 100 miles out in blue-water fishing-- for Marlin.

The Snook Whisper's fishing vessel, an unnamed boat, lay at anchor off the beautiful, blue-green waters of Bahia Honda, on the Atlantic side of the keys.

The Old Salt was already there waiting for me on the dock at first light. We set out, not with but into the rising sun.

He smiles and hands me a huge 14 Aut reel and rod- tools of the trade for landing a very large fish, what I have come out here for.

I sit on the bow as we set out for the Loop current, the salt spray whipping my face. It is cold and it stings, awakening me to early dawn.

Further out, I see the frigate birds and sea-turtles.

Upon our approach, the sea-turtle does not dive, and the Old Salt informs me that this is unnatural; it must be ill. As we pass by, riding the waves I observe tumors on its face around its beak, which signals that it is indeed sick and trying to heal itself on the surface.

Further out, after the many hurricanes, amid howling gales at sea- a strange sight greets our eyes- a dead cow floating by, upside down, its legs perpendicular, its belly bloated, in the long trail of sea grass.

A large, translucent Cassiopeia jellyfish glides by, a swirling, pulsing nebula of color and light, its long tendrils reaching down to the depths. It's the most beautiful thing I've ever seen.

Or so I thought. At sea there are many wonders.

An Eagle Ray, brown and white spotted, glides by, it's wingspan at least six feet, on its way to some distant destination. At depth, under a blue-green wave, it is astonishingly beautiful as it moves like a thing from another world.

One hundred miles out from any sign of land, 1,800 feet down, the water is a deep, iridescent, peacock blue, translucent as an eye wide open, the yellow rays of sunlight flickering among the undulating shadows of the iris. One can only guess how deep it is, or what's down there.

The steady rocking motion of the waves, back and forth, the constant pitching up and down, is a like a slow measured movement, an adagio for strings, the violins hitting the high notes, a cello in the lower register. Out here there is nothing but time and space, and time has slowed to a crawl. I feel it in my heartbeat-there is no time anymore. No past, no future, only the present. Time is a fictional construct: seconds, minutes, hours, days, weeks, months, years- all man-made. There is only the eternal now, and I am living in it. Waiting…

It's ironic our boat has no name, for there are no words to express the sense of loneliness, the utter isolation of the open ocean. It's beyond the power of words.

A landlessness of rolling sea, waves that tower in the distance, touching the clouds, and rock and pitch under our little boat, wandering endlessly toward a distant horizon, which is the only sense of realism you have out here, other than the sun and stars to ground you. Gravity seems not to apply, as the deck shifts beneath your feet. Otherwise you are completely alone with your thoughts.

I'm worried about my father. In spite of my best efforts, he's not getting better. He continues to grow weaker, more feeble by the day; he has a moldering look about him. Most days, he huddles in his wheel chair, his face bent down, arms slumped at his side. It looks like he's losing the fight. He's even stopped walking with his walker, and stays in bed and watches TV most days. "They're all waiting on the other side," he mutters darkly. It won't be long."

"Let's get up," I say, go outside and take a walk. It's a beautiful day."

"Not today," he says and turns his face to the wall.

"Don't give up, dad," I'd say, something stinging my eyes.

"Fish on, father. Fish on!"

In furtherance of the dream, I bought an antique marlin lure, from the 1920's. Probably like something Hemingway used. It looks like a squid, crafted from hard-carved wood, painted black, with big yellow eyes, a black and purple rubber skirt, hiding the hook.

The Old Salt expertly rigs it for me.

"Better get in the fighting chair," he suggests. "We're going to start trolling."

"No," I say. I want to stand and fight it. To feel its power."

He shakes his head and guns the engine, but I think he understands and secretly approves.

Following the weed lines along the flight of a lone Frigate Bird, we drift over a bright patch of blue swells, trolling for Marlin with my lure, its black and blue skirt, skipping in and out of our wake.

Suddenly, the pole twists into a pretzel-- like it is going to snap in half as the brute strength and awesome power of something incredibly large at the other end, brings me to my knees.

It is unbelievably heavy. Immovable. It wrenches my back out and my arms begin to shake just trying to hold it up. Afterwards, I will sleep on my stomach for a week.

Before the Old Salt can do or say anything, the rod and reel are ripped right out of my hands. It ricochets across the deck, bounces to the bow, smashes into the gun-whale, and hurtles into the sea like a bottle rocket shot out of a coke bottle.

"Big, big fish" the Old Salt muses laconically. "Like the old days off Cuba."

I'm in utter shock- I can't believe what just happened. So sudden and unexpected, the big fish and the big dream, both gone. Snatched right out of my hands. Did I come all this way to lose everything? My father, the fish, my dream?

No, I learned the most valuable lesson of all. The lesson of the Marlin. There are forces too powerful, too vast and too out of reach, which will forever remain beyond our control. God --death, a big blue marlin, they bring us to our knees, humbling us. I felt small out there on the vast, blue, rolling sea, in the presence of a power greater than I.

I was vulnerable, overwhelmed and unprepared when the true test came, but I tried—I did my best, and in the end, the struggle was worth it, especially for a shot at big blue marlin, the largest, grandest and brightest of all big dreams. There was nothing I could do, the fish was too big; I had to let go. I could not hold on. This then was my destiny.

In the end, I could not save my father either.

I feel an existential emptiness, cut off from easy answers. I'm adrift at sea in more ways than one. It is a feeling of exposure. My theatrical heroics, my stubborn desire to overcome and succeed on a superficial level- all have been in vain.

I am alone and without hope, except for the self-reliance I have picked up from fishing, but at least that is something. There are no drugs to cure my malaise, nor alcohol to stop my free-fall into oblivion. Nothing but who I am. A fisherman who does not quit.

As we head for home, I see Venus twinkling in the night sky. The lunar cycle is at last complete. From birth to death, from quarter moon to half and full again, the seasons of life change, and I must change with them. A million stars are out, shining on the sea.

I have hooked my first and last big fish, and feel a little like Alexander the Great who, upon conquering the known world, sat down and wept because there were no more worlds left to conquer.

But I went out deep; I gave it my all. I stood my ground in the things that really matter: the big things in life like death and love, and a big, big fish, and inevitably I lost, but I did not back down. I went down on my knees in the midnight hour, and found there is a power greater than I, a power deeper, higher, wider and vaster than I.

Ever since men and women have dreamed big dreams, they have endured and suffered for them—and I have suffered too, but I did not run. I fought and fished on, for fishing is a thing of the spirit, and big dreams come true only if you are willing to go out deep, deeper than you ever thought you could, deep into blue water 100 miles from any land, to face what must be faced - alone. The existential questions of existence. I am the existential angler.

27 Calling The Spirit Down: I, Fisherman

–Coda

I call the spirit of the first fisherman, of all fishermen, down. I ask their blessing.

13,000 B.C. Archeological evidence of the earliest fishermen, dated to the Pre Ceramic history of South America, has been excavated from a myriad of small fishing villages along the coast of South America, all the way down to Tierra Del Fuego on the tip of Cape Horn.

Artifacts discovered inside the half-buried fishermens' huts include the shredded remnants of cotton netting, with gourds attached to hold the nets afloat, the bones of Spanish Sardines, by the thousands, a strand of fishing line, tied with a knot, curved shell hooks and the ritualistic drawings of sea birds on the walls of one of the huts.

The intimate details of the lives of early fisherman, part of a distinguished lecture series in a power-point presentation at Eckerd College, in the Marine Science Center, are so much more than academic. They touch something deep inside. For through these specific exemplars, the early fishermen live again.

As the Professor, from the University of Maine, clicked through the slides, I was caught up in the lives of the fishermen going about their daily routine. They arose early, prayed to their fishing gods, tied their knots, mended their nets, and set out to challenge the elements, to feed their families and to bring home the big fish.

Today, modern fishing is more of a recreational sport, yet hang around the docks and bridges, the jetties and marinas long enough, and you will observe many fisherman who are still engaged in the epic struggle to wrest a living from the sea.

They travel backwards in a long, unending line of fishermen—the first to cast out a line into the vast unconquered continent of a new world in its primeval state.

It was and is a proud tradition with respect among the honorable fisherman of all times, for the delicate balance of the ecosystem.

Only the commercial fishing industry, with its corporate avarice, dragging miles of gill-nets through the sea, like a strip-mining operation, breaks with this grand tradition, jeopardizing many of the greatest game-fish that swim the seas: the Marlin, the Tuna and the Swordfish. Although gill-nets have been banned in Florida, the industry continues its widespread use, decimating the Leatherback Sea-turtle and other essential species critical to the procreation of the sea and its marine life.

It is a vicious cycle.

When the Leatherback is caught at depth, it cannot get back to the surface and drowns. The Leatherback feeds on gelatinous invertebrates, otherwise known as jellyfish. The jellyfish eat the larval Marlin, Tuna and Swordfish before they mature. Without a proper understanding of the cycle of life in the sea, the delicate balance of nature is upset and the great blue-water denizens of the deep are becoming endangered by man's greed. Imagine an ocean without the Marlin, Tuna or Swordfish.

The ancient fishermen took only what they needed to feed themselves and their families. They were good stewards of the earth and sea and all its resources.

In my mind's eye I see them casting out their nets, hung with gourds, not for sustenance alone, like the bones of Spanish Sardines unearthed near their huts, but to catch bait-fish as well—for other larger fish must've loomed around the dark clouds of Sardines in the water. One immediately comes to mind, a fish that loves Spanish Sardines —the Snook.

I see one fisherman in particular, slipping a carved shell hook onto his line, tying the knot fast. A knot, which will outlast the pyramids—that will see the rise and fall of the Roman Empire, that ushered in the Dark Ages and the Renaissance, that saw a man walk on the moon. A knot tied to hold and never break. A knot 13,000 years old. A knot like that was tied for bigger fish than Spanish Sardines.

He must've been a bit of a dreamer, for only one knot, one shell hook and one drawing of a sea-bird has been found among the ruined huts on the beaches of South America. He must've been a man of character and substance, a fisherman among fisherman, for he alone, among the other villagers, went out deeper, where the big fish swim.

I know fisherman. Then as now, I see them standing on the shore, scanning the horizon, through their polarized sunglasses, for signs of seabirds. They cast out their nets and pull them up, loaded with Spanish Sardines—whitebait as it is called, quivering in the sun like quick-silver. While the women and children clean the nets, the lone fisherman stands out from among the rest. Arising at dawn, he plucked a charred cinder from among the glowing embers of the hearth.

He knelt inside his hut and bowed his head, then etched an icon upon the walls of his hut, that which he knew would draw the fish to his shell-hook—the seabird.

But he was searching for much more than tiny Sardines, for he had seen, among the dark cloud in the water, the wakes of larger fish on the periphery of his preternatural sight. His vision saw beyond what was to what could be, and as the other fishermen were busily scooping up their daily diet of Spanish Sardines, he waded out a little further than the rest, to where the sea-birds flocked beyond the blue-breakers, to cast out his shell-hook and line.

The line with the knot he tied that very morning as he knelt to draw the seabird on his wall—a knot to outlast the millennia to come – and he caught and landed something no one had ever caught before—a big fish, perhaps a Snook, a Redfish, a Speckled Trout or Pompano. I wonder if his heart skipped a beat when he felt the tug on the end of the line and his knot came under the trial of a big fish, and if he smiled in satisfaction as it held?

I see the people of the village gathered 'round in awe and wonder, only guessing by what special magic the fisherman had done this? How could they know, those early fisherman, who dreamed only of Sardines to feed their bellies, that one among them had visions of larger fish, bigger dreams, to feed something in his heart and spirit. It must've been an evolutionary leap forward on that day. The big fish could feed his family for a week, perhaps even the entire village. I see him rise, and look to sea, and in a flash, the probability of cause and effect summons his curiosity. It is the Spanish Sardines, their daily diet from time immemorial, which the big fish seek. He tests his knot, pulling it tight with his teeth. He gathers up his net and casts out. Concentric ripples propel outward into the future.

Fishing from the shore of Pass-A-Grille, I am drawn back with the ancient fishermen all the way to Atlantis.

My net is full and I open it upon the shore, and spill my catch of Spanish Sardines into a bait bucket. The sun-fire is setting, and day is drawing to a close. The new moon, like the semi-circle of a fisherman's carved shell hook, trolls amid a multitude of stars, which swim like a school of baitfish across the sky.

Fish On!

The seasons have turned and brought with it springtime. The warm sea breeze caresses my face.

The tide is high.

The sea is teeming with life, clouds of bait-fish, schools of Snook, dolphin and other game fish. Over my shoulder nestled among the palms, stands my little fishing cottage. A fire beckons from the open door of my hut. My wife is calling…

My son and daughter accompany me down by the shore. They are growing impatient, chasing their shadows among the realms of gold. They wait for me to quit.

But I do not quit. Not yet. The sea is calling. My eyes stray toward the horizon as a flock of seabirds gather. From careful observation and experience, I know what that means. Big fish leap and prey upon the smaller fish—everywhere the sea is roiled. I sharpen my shell-hook and cast out one last time—instantly I get a hook-up, then another and another. I drag them up onto the shore and lay them out side by side.

I see a man walking jauntily down the beach towards me, a torch-light in his hand. I blink once, then twice—it's the Old Salt, the master fisherman who taught me everything I know—only now he's so darkly tanned he looks like an Indian. He passes by and his eyes twinkle in the dusk, the shadow of a smile upon the corners of his mouth. He whispers the secret name, or is it the wind?

"Fish on brother," he says and hands me the torch in passing. And then I hear the bells…and I am drawn back.

My children race out of the shadows to see what I have caught. Three big Snook. Three big smiles. For they enjoy the clean bright taste of Snook, and are heartily weary of the oily taste of sardines. We will eat well tonight.

I take my children's hands. We stroll home together through the lengthening shadows, between the fringed plams, leaning into the sunset, leaving a trail of footprints in the sand, which the incoming tide will wash away, as if we'd never walked this shore.

The storms have passed. I have left civilization and all its troubles behind. A woven grass stringer, laden with fish to feed my family, is strung across my shoulder. My wife stands at the doorway beckoning. I am barefoot, sunburned and happy. I am a fisherman.

I am the Snook Whisperer now.

Fish on-

--Pass-A-Grille, 2007

THE END

Acknoledgements:

The author wishes to thank John and Christine Tortorella for their interest in this fishing book. As a world champion coach and tournament fisherman, Coach Tortorella's commentary is invaluable. And to my dear friend Chris, my special thanks for everything. Cover photo: Dr. Thomas Smith.

Sloane W. Golden has published in newspapers, magazines and journals. As a writer, professor and fishing guide, Mr. Golden publishes a monthly fishing column in the Island Reporter, under the by-line, The Existential Angler. He currently has a screenplay about Jimi Hendix making waves in Hollywood as well as a television fishing show, of the same name as the book, in the works.

LaVergne, TN USA
01 September 2009

156608LV00002B/3/P